Norm Clarke's **VEGAS CONFIDENTIAL:**

Sinsational Celebrity Tales

Stephens Press ▪ Las Vegas, Nevada

Editor: Mike Weatherford
Copy editor: Jamie Carpenter
Designer: Sue Campbell
Photo Editor: Stacey Fott
Cover photos: Vegas Strip by Jon Sullivan, Norm's photo by Jeff Scheid

Cataloging-in-Publication
Clarke, Norm.
    Norm Clarke's Vegas confidential : sinsational celebrity tales / Norm Clarke ; [edited by] Mike Weatherford.
    272 p. : photos ; 14 cm.

A compilation of stories about the celebrities who visit and live in Las Vegas from Clarke's entertainment column that appears in the Las Vegas Review-Journal
ISBN: 1-932173-77-3
ISBN-13: 978-1-932173-77-2

1. Celebrities—Anecdotes. 2. Celebrities—Nevada—Las Vegas—Anecdotes. I.Title II. Title: Sinsational celebrity tales. III. Title: Vegas confidential.

979.3/135/033 dc22   2009   2007938112

STEPHENS PRESS, LLC
A Stephens Media Company

Post Office Box 1600
Las Vegas, NV 89125-1600
www.stephenspress.com

Printed in Hong Kong

Contents

Foreword

The first time I met Norm Clarke, he confessed that he thought I was a mob guy. Not long afterwards, *The Sopranos* agreed.

I've lived in Las Vegas for 25 years and I can tell you the idea of a gossip columnist covering our town wasn't immediately embraced. But Norm's style and accuracy quickly made him the "Page Six" of Las Vegas. When I open the *Review-Journal*, the first thing I turn to is Norm — just like most of the locals.

Whether it's a national story or a juicy local angle, Norm gets it and gets it right. I'm not quite sure how he does it, but he doesn't miss a thing.

When you're in Vegas and you want to know who's where, who's been there, and what they did, check out Norm's "Vegas Confidential." He's been a terrific friend to the city — and to the cast of *The Sopranos*. When Tony (Paulie Walnuts) Sirico met Norm for the first time, he said, "I'd hate to see what the other guy looks like."

Let me give it to you straight: You haven't made it in Vegas until you've made Norm's column.

—Steve Schirripa, *The Sopranos*

Above: Steve Schirripa
Photo: Courtesy Caesars Palace

Acknowledgements

In the dot-dot-dot style to which I've become accustomed, I raise a glass to those who had so much to do with making this book happen. . . .

To *Las Vegas Review-Journal* entertainment writer Mike Weatherford, who edited this book and the predecessor, *Vegas Confidential: 1,000 Naked Truths*, with extraordinary skill, creativity, and boundless patience. Oh, to have Mike's talent for one week. . . .

To Cara Roberts, a.k.a. "The Leggy Blonde," for your love and all those nights of *Project Runway* and *Top Chef* that you gave up to be the best Girl Friday any columnist could ask for. And for bringing the joy of Rumor and Scandal into our lives. . . .

To *Las Vegas Review-Journal* publisher Sherm Frederick, for giving me the opportunity to write this kind of a column in the most exciting city in the world, and to *Las Vegas Review-Journal* attorney Mark Hinueber, for his ever-sound advice and support. . . .

To Dr. Stephen Miller, whose incredible professionalism allowed me to stay healthy long enough to add some "bonus" years to covering a city I adore. . . .

To my brother Jeff Scheid, George Maloof, Robin Leach, Michele Jaffe, Frank Lieberman, Barry Forbis, Andrew Hudson, David McReynolds, Ira David Sternberg, Aaron Alexander, and the late Randy Rutherford and Joe Stein, for their friendship and inspiration. . . .

To Ray Frank, Bud Hickey, Gordie Spear, Bill Spiller, Wick Temple, Paul Freeman, and Bill Winter, for giving me the early breaks. To Denny Dressman, for getting me to Denver and giving me the opportunity of a lifetime

— covering a big league team from scratch. To Melanie Dressman for all that home cooking. A special thanks to the late Herb Caen, the master of man-about-town columns. . . .

Finally, to the many dedicated PR people, special contributors (yes, that means bouncers, strippers, and valets), loyal readers, and former assistant Jeremy Pond, who collectively made me look good by keeping a river of information flowing into my laptop and Blackberry.

—Norm Clarke

Introduction

This is my second book, and I'm going to be damn careful who gets a book this time.

Four years ago, Stephens Press also published *Vegas Confidential: 1,000 Naked Truths*, which was based on my *Las Vegas Review-Journal* column. Soon after its publication, baseball great Pete Rose invited me to lunch and I passed him a copy of the book at Smith & Wollensky. It was my first contact with him since spring training of 1989, just before Major League Baseball announced it was investigating him for unspecified "serious allegations" which turned out to be betting on baseball.

Rose and I have a long, checkered history. I had covered the Cincinnati Reds during their heyday, when they won consecutive world championships in 1975 and 1976. I was the lead sportswriter in the Cincinnati Associated Press office from 1973 to late 1978.

During those six years of covering the Reds, there were few people in sports more colorful than Pete Rose. One day he'd fill your notebook with killer quotes, and a week later, after revealing too much in an interview, he'd throw a wet towel in your face and growl, "Don't write that!"

The angriest he got at me was during the 1976 National League Championship Series. I found out that negotiations with the Reds had reached an impasse and that Rose told his attorney, "If I'm too rich for their blood they can trade my ass to the Phillies."

I wrote the story and the stuff hit the fan. Pete threatened to punch my "headlights" out the next day when I went up to him at the batting cage, after he told WKRC-TV anchorman Nick Clooney (George's dad) that my story was "hogwash, with a capital H-O-G."

Rose's ex-wife, Carolyn, later told me, "I've only seen Pete mad enough to kill someone once, and that was when you wrote the negotiations story."

Years later, I broke the story that Rose was planning to announce his retirement. The next morning, I turned on ESPN and Pete was not only denying it, but he added, "That guy in Denver has never got anything right."

A couple of hours later, he made his retirement official.

So, fast-forward to present-day Las Vegas and my first dinner with Internet guru Matt Drudge, who had just linked my newspaper column to his *DrudgeReport.com.* We were starting dinner at N9NE when I heard Drudge say, "Norm, that was Pete Rose walking by."

I looked up and saw Pete 15 feet away, walking toward the exit. I called out his name twice and he didn't respond. With all the noise and so many voices calling out to him on a daily basis, I assumed it was a case of one or the other.

Below: Pete Rose and Norm have a history.
Photo: Marlene Karas/ *Review-Journal*

As he was walking toward the hostess area, the N9NE general manager mouthed the words to me, "Do you want to talk to him?" When I nodded affirmatively, the GM said something to Pete, who turned around and gave me the old parade wave, like the Pope, and a sort of forced, up-yours smile.

He turned away and kept walking. That's odd, I thought. We had just had lunch, at his invitation, ten days earlier, and now he doesn't have time to say hello?

I had no sooner turned back to Drudge and Cara, when I noticed Pete was walking toward our table, the first one on the left as you walk in. I stood up to shake hands and make introductions, when he reached up and slapped me across the face with his right hand.

"What the hell!" I said.

"You made me the 'No. 5' worst tipper in your fuckin' book," he said before turning away and heading for the door.

You should have seen the look on Drudge's face.

"Did he just slap you?"

"Yes."

"What was that all about?" Drudge asked.

Well, umm, I forgot that I gave him my book. And, umm, when I gave him the book it might also have slipped my mind that, yes, he was mentioned among the top ten worst tippers in town; page 72, if you have a copy.

At that moment, I heard the voice of George Maloof, owner and operator of the Palms. "Norm, this is Tom Brady."

The bitch-slapping had happened maybe 20–30 seconds earlier and I thought the casino boss and the New England Patriots' quarterback must have witnessed it.

I asked George, "Did you see what just happened?"

"No," he said.

"Pete Rose just slapped me over something I wrote about him."

Brady's jaw dropped. "Pete Rose just slapped you?!" He looked over at Maloof and back at me. They were exchanging that Damn! How'd-we-miss-that? look.

After I recounted the incident in my column a day later, I got a call from a buddy in Denver.

"Hey, congratulations," chirped Mark Wolf, a former colleague at the *Rocky Mountain News*.

"For what?" I said.

"You're in the Hall of Fame," said Wolfie. "You gave up Pete Rose's last hit."

Chapter 1 – Hey Big Spender

The Gilded Age of Las Vegas arrived about the same time as boxer Floyd Mayweather, Jr.

He stood out as the perfect poster child for a wild-spending era that makes the Roaring Twenties look tamer than a church social.

Nobody rolls like Mayweather. One night in October 2007 said it all, when he showed up at Wynn Las Vegas in his Maybach, with his entourage right behind in a Mercedes SLR McLaren and a Rolls-Royce Phantom, each worth about $500,000.

Around Mayweather's neck were twin diamond pendants shaped like boxing gloves and studded with rubies. In his back pocket was $15,000 to $20,000 in cash, "rain" money to shower on the chichi crowd at Wynn's Tryst nightclub.

He's no lightweight at the strip clubs, either. On another night, Mayweather dropped $50,000 in tips at one of his favorite skin joints.

Anyone who spent much time at OPM (now Poetry), a hotspot at the Forum Shops at Caesars Palace, likely shared in Mayweather's largesse. "I've seen him (make it rain) at least 20 times in the last couple years," said Branden Powers, Poetry's marketing director and part owner.

"With me it's entertainment," Mayweather told me on the eve of his December 2007 fight with Ricky Hatton.

"We're in the entertainment capital of the world," Mayweather said. "Why not bring something different to the sport — flash and flair."

Opposite page: Welterweight boxing champion Floyd Mayweather, Jr. walks into Tryst nightclub (Wynn) holding bundles of cash that he uses to "make it rain," a practice that got its name from bills being showered on nightclub crowds. Mayweather is known for regularly "making it rain" at a number of Las Vegas nightclubs and adult entertainment clubs. *Photo:* Courtesy Tryst

"When you watch Floyd Mayweather," he said, "you don't just see a guy who entertains — a guy that's flamboyant — but also a kid who has a heart and who gives back to the community, to kids who are less fortunate."

Said Powers, "I've seen him buying out Nike Town, with 20 to 30 bags of shoes in tow."

With all that flash and cash, some worried that he was courting trouble.

Not Powers. "He travels with more muscle than John Gotti did."

A new contender

Boxer Zab Judah took the bottle-buying binge to breathtaking heights in January 2008 at Prive, the new club at Planet Hollywood Resort.

After Mayweather bought three magnums of Perrier-Jouët Rose champagne and tossed $5,000 into the dance floor crowd, Judah made his own statement by ordering 50 bottles of Dom Perignon at $1,000 a bottle.

More bottle-swinging

Getting Kobe Bryant to back down will win you points in basketball and the macho world of poker. But Bryant wasn't playing either when he manned up against poker player Antonio Esfandiari in the art of nightclub one-upsmanship.

After being invited to hang out with Vegas power couple Steve and Elaine Wynn, Bryant and his wife, Vanessa, made a rare nightspot appearance when they attended the opening night

Below: Poker player Antonio Esfandiari, winner of the Blush nightclub show-down.
Photo: Christine H. Wetzel/ *Review-Journal*

of the Blush boutique nightclub at Wynn Las Vegas in September 2007.

Seated directly across from Esfandiari, Bryant watched as the poker pro ordered a bottle of Cristal champagne.

"Every time someone orders a bottle of champagne we come up with a movie theme song," said Blush honcho Sean Christie. "We play *Rocky*, *James Bond*, or *Mission Impossible*. Dramatic music and sparklers.

"Kobe saw that and asked that we play *Rocky*. He bought five bottles of Cristal, and when we bring them out, Antonio orders another five.

"Kobe goes, 'Oh no, hell no,' and says, 'Give me ten more bottles.'"

When the bubbly arrived, Esfandiari and his friend ordered 20 more. The next day, Esfandiari went to gossip website *TMZ.com*, saying he outspent Kobe and showed them a receipt for $35,000. Kobe's was $21,000.

On second thought

When is a big tip too big? A cocktail server in the VIP section at Pure nightclub inside Caesars Palace freaked out when a customer gave her a $50,000 tip. She refused the cash bonanza, much to the chagrin of the other two girls on her VIP team. But after getting an earful from her two co-workers, she had a change of heart. When she returned to the high roller's table, she agreed to a $20,000 tip.

Easy come, easy go

Massive NFL party hound Ross Verba cut a wide swath in Las Vegas with his easy come, easy go spirit.

While partying past dawn at ICE, the since-closed off-Strip nightclub popularized in the reality show, *The*

What'ya Wanna Bet?

Hockey Icon Wayne Gretsky came under scrutiny after his wife, Janet Jones, was implicated in a sports betting ring days before the 2006 Winter Olympics opened.

A source told me that the hockey great has lost more than $2 million in MGM Mirage properties. Gretsky, then head coach of the Phoenix Coyotes, had a credit line at the time that allowed him to bet up to $25,000 per hand. But he plays well below that level, my source said. Gretsky's wife normally plays $1,000 a hand.

Blackjack is their game of choice, and they usually play in the MGM Grand Mansion, where guests must risk $250,000 over two or three days to stay in the high roller suites. She was under investigation for betting more than $500,000 in sports bets, including $75,000 on the Super Bowl.

Left: Hockey great Wayne Gretsky enjoys playing blackjack.
Photo: ⊚Håkan Dahlström

Club, the Green Bay Packers' offensive lineman knew how to keep the party going.

"Tiesto, who was the No. 1 deejay in the world at the time, was playing, and $10,000 in cash came raining down in the deejay booth and we went another 90 minutes, until 10 a.m.," said Brian Klimaski, director of VIP services.

That same year, 2005, the 300-pound offensive lineman went on a legendary champagne binge after winning a reported half-million dollars at the Palms. Verba, a free spirit, blew most of it, I was told, on a "massive champagne buying/spraying spree" at Green Valley Ranch's pool party known as Nirvana.

During the party at his cabana, he recruited seven bikini-clad babes for a "hot body" contest, and rather than picking a single winner, he awarded each of the entries $10,000 for participating.

A month later, Verba was back in town, tossing $800 in one dollar bills into the crowd and at the go-go girls at ICE. He was overheard offering the ICE deejay $7,000 to play an extra hour.

Something to remember him by

A member of the Las Vegas Pussycat Dolls made quite an impression on an admirer. Although she never went out with the man, she agreed to accept a gift from him. He instructed her to meet him outside the main entrance at Caesars Palace, where, on top of a flatbed truck near the limo area, a new BMW awaited.

Fatburger mystery man

I receive dozens of calls or emails a year about high rollers who leave mind-boggling tips to the dealers or the service industry. The odds of me knowing one would be slimmer than slim.

One night in 2000, an MGM Grand limo pulled up at

Above: Step away from the grill!

Photo: ©Matthias Zirngibl/Tscherno

the Fatburger across from the Monte Carlo at about 4 a.m., and a well-dressed man in his 40s came in for his favorite burger. Having just won a huge amount of money at Bellagio, his exuberance — or the alcohol — got the best of him and suddenly he was behind the counter impersonating a fry cook.

When the manager ordered the customer out of the cooking area, the apologetic high-roller reached into a bulging envelope, and handed over a $100 bill.

He didn't stop with the manager. He passed C-notes to the rest of the employees on the graveyard shift and then walked around the restaurant, passing out hundreds to dumbstruck patrons.

The postscript to the story came about five years later. I was in Tabu Ultra Lounge at the MGM Grand when an old friend from my Denver sportswriting days walked up with a stunning gal pal and said hello.

After a few minutes of conversation, his lady friend turned to him and said, "Can I tell him?"

She asked me if I recalled the story I had written about the big tipper at Fatburger.

"Of course," I said.

Pointing to my friend, she said, "That was Charlie."

It was Charlie Monfort, co-owner of the Colorado Rockies.

Repeat business

The VIP servers at Tao inside The Venetian can't wait to see a certain big spender: He tipped over $150,000 within the first two years that the mega-club was open.

Another Tao customer tipped $24,000, and three weeks later, toked another $22,000. An NBA player promised one of Tao's cocktail servers that he would be back to see her the following week and gave her his $25,000-plus diamond-studded watch as collateral.

If we could do it all again

Las Vegas attorney Jim Jimmerson and his wife Carol didn't have to go all the way to Venice to renew their wedding vows on their tenth anniversary. They went to St. Mark's Square at The Venetian for a romantic Renaissance-themed renewal on February 15, 2002. It included a canal ride on a golden wedding gondola to St. Mark's Square, with strolling musicians performing along the way.

As they glided under the last arch on the canal, 25,000 rose petals rained down on them from basket-bearing women in gowns from the Renaissance era. Fog rose from the canal as they reached the dock,

where they were greeted with songs from women in costumes. Most of the 150 guests watched from nearby canal bridges. It was the first wedding allowed at The Venetian Grand Canal Shops at St. Mark's Square.

Yao!

Chinese New Year might not be the best time to take human silo Yao Ming, the Houston Rockets' seven-foot six-inch All-Star center, to Wing Lei, the opulent Chinese restaurant at Wynn Las Vegas.

Below: Dinner with Yao Ming could amount to serious yen.
Photo: Kevork Djansezian/AP

When Chinese New Year kicked off in February 2007, Wing Lei offered a three-tiered menu that started at $198, jumped to $388 for the midrange option and topped out at $988.

Chef Richard Chen went over his shopping list with

me: dried Japanese abalone, $2,226 a pound; bird's nest for bird's nest soup, $1,600 a pound (an ounce of bird's nest goes into a bowl of bird's nest soup, which fetches $90); and spotted grouper from Southeast Asia, which sells for $225 on the menu.

Chen said it's not unusual for a large Chinese family to spend $20,000 to $30,000 on a dinner. With fine wine, he's seen dinner checks soar to $50,000.

Command performance

Around Las Vegas, Michael Jordan has a well-deserved reputation as a tightwad extraordinaire: "Hoardin' Jordan," they call him. But some fans would dispute that. When The Roots finished performing at the Hard Rock Hotel during NBA All-Star Weekend of 2007, it was

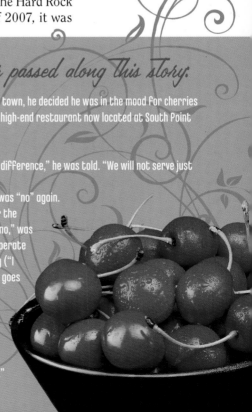

An out-of-Town high roller passed along this story:

After dining at one of the more popular restaurants in town, he decided he was in the mood for cherries jubilee. Aware they were on the menu at Michael's, the high-end restaurant now located at South Point Hotel and Casino, he put in a call.

He was told Michael's does not serve "*just dessert.*"

He offered $500 for a single order. "Money makes no difference," he was told. "We will not serve just dessert to anyone."

The high roller upped the ante to $5,000. The answer was "no" again.

He offered to order an entire dinner to go except for the dessert, which he wanted to eat at Michael's. "No and no," was the answer. Undeterred, the caller made one more desperate try; he said he was an agent for a well-known celebrity ("I gave no name") who wanted the cherries jubilee, which goes for $22 per person.

"No means no," he was told.

"That's a true story," confirmed Jose Martell, the maitre d' at Michael's. "It's been a long-standing policy. It would tie up the table and it's a losing proposition. We can't have someone come in here for a salad."

announced the band would be playing a second show. Insiders say it was Jordan who coughed up big bucks for the encore performance, which ended after 2 a.m.

Wait here – really!

A limo driver emailed me one night in 2006 with a story about a high-profile fare. Upon delivering the 40-something passenger to his home in a tony gated community, the fare apologized and said he didn't have enough money on him. The limo driver had been down that road before with many a ride. The passenger asked the driver to wait a minute while he headed for his house. When he returned, Palms owner George Maloof handed over a $400 tip.

That same year, somebody from Maloof's party flipped a $1,000 chip onto the stage during lounge band Sunset Strip's set at the Las Vegas Hilton. The chip was tossed to singer Lorena Peril after her version of Christina Aguilera's "Beautiful."

Playgirl shopping

Paris Hilton's prodigious shopping prowess was on full display at the Palms during the 2006 opening weekend of the Playboy Club in the new Fantasy Tower. Maloof, in a show of appreciation for her loyalty, took her shopping and added, "Get whatever you want and something for Nicky." Forty-five minutes later, the hotel heiress left with two diamond-studded watches worth $50,000 each, three Bunny necklaces, and a Bunny belly ring.

But money can't buy everything

Rappers Lil' Flip and Chamillionaire wanted entrance into OPM (now Poetry), the popular nightclub adjacent to Caesars Palace, so badly

Below: Paris Hilton at Jet Nightclub. The girl can shop.
Photo: Cara Roberts

that they offered to pay $20,000 for 20 magnums of expensive Cristal champagne.

They were refused entry for not meeting the club's dress-code standards.

A Wynn-win situation

Sometimes it all goes to a good cause.

A high roller at Wynn caught an early case of the Christmas spirit in 2006. After winning $500,000 in the winner-take-all blackjack tournament, he gave it all to charity. A Wynn rep said the high roller, who did not want to be identified, donated the windfall to The Cystic Fibrosis Foundation and the J.F. Shea Therapeutic Riding Center.

Buying a round – a really big round

You'd think running up a $30,000 drink tab would be enough fun for one night. Not for a high roller who decided to show some love to the entire crowd at Tao nightclub at The Venetian. He ordered shots for everyone, which came to another $10,000, when management gave him a deal: 2,000 shots at $5 each.

Happy New Year

The free-money frenzy took on a different twist on New Year's Eve 2007 when a non-celebrity got involved.

Reginald Thomas, occupation unknown, called the Poetry club and said he wanted to come in and "make it rain."

He showed up wearing a backpack stuffed with bricks of bills and got the party started by tossing out $5,000 worth in cash at midnight. He continued to shower the bills all night.

"I even saw him throw bricks of $1 bills into the crowd, not even taking the time to separate them," said Branden Powers, the club's marketing director.

Michael Jordan
Photo: Clint Karlsen / Review-Journal

Michael Bolton
Photo: Kevork Djansezian/AP

Jaleel White
Photo: Christine H. Wetzell / Review-Journal

Joe Francis
Photo: Mark J. Terril/AP

Michael Vick
Photo: Haraz N. Ghanbari/AP

Terrell Owens
Photo: Tim Sharp/AP

Sylvester Stallone
Photo: Tom Donoghue/Courtesy Planet Hollywood

Britney Spears
Photo: ©FriPaparazzi

Donovan McNabb
Photo: Joseph Kaczmarek/ AP

Sugar Ray Leonard
Photo: Courtesy Planet Hollywood

Chapter 2 – Good Tippers, Bad Tippers, and Cheap Bastards

know what some of you are thinking. Since Pete Rose bitch-slapped me for including him in my worst tippers list in my last book, you're wondering if he's going to be a re-Pete.

That would be a yes. In October 2007, Rose, talking to Las Vegas freelance journalist Steve Friess on *TheStripPodcast.com*, said he would cough up $100 to anyone who caught him gambling.

Had the former Cincinnati Reds star, who was banned from baseball for gambling, turned over a new leaf? Not according to the sports book employees who fired off emails or made phone calls to me the next day.

"He always uses runners to make his bets or collect on them," said one. "He has runners so he doesn't have to tip," was another's theory.

And if Rose is paying his minions for placing his bets or collecting, "that's not allowed under Nevada gaming regulations," according to a Las Vegas sports book operator. "If someone's being paid, we're not allowed to take those bets."

Hitting below the (money) belt

Sometimes leaving nothing is better than the third option: the cheap-ass, why-bother insult of a tip. Sylvester Stallone was in town for the finale of his boxing reality-TV series, *The Contender*. He camped out for hours with some palookas at one of the big clubs, running up a drink tab of $5,000 to $6,000. When Pure picked up the tab, the server got a whopping $5 tip.

Opposite page: The Cheapskates Hall of Shame.

'Keep the change'

Jaleel White, better known as Steve Urkel, America's favorite nerd on TV's *Family Matters*, took a cab from the Wynn to Bellagio and gave the cabbie a 20-cent tip on a fare of $7.80.

Cold cash

Michael Jordan and Wayne Gretzky were playing at the same blackjack table one night, firing large chips. Jordan, suffering from a bad head cold, asked his cocktail server if she would get him an antihistamine. When she returned with the medicine, Gretzky politely nudged Jordan, saying "Give her a little something." When Jordan ignored him, Gretzky put a $25 chip on her drink tray. Jordan reached over and picked up the chip and returned it to Gretzky's pile. Then he coughed up a $5 chip.

Celine's love boat hits iceberg

Celine Dion hosted a birthday party for her mother aboard the $1,295-an-hour *La Contessa* yacht at Lake Las Vegas Resort. After days of preparation, $10,000 in catering, and a staff of ten to serve 20 guests, the staff and crew got zilch. "It appeared that Celine was more concerned about carrying off a tray of left-over chocolates than thanking the staff for their service," said my spy.

Not amused

Boxing legend "Sugar" Ray Leonard had just made millions the night before in a Las Vegas title fight when he decided to test his luck at blackjack. He got hot and was up about $8,000, but none of it was going to the Harrah's dealers or cocktail servers. At one point, a fellow player said to him, "Aren't you going to give the dealer something?" My spy said Leonard's response was to pull out a picture of himself, autograph it, and hand it to a dealer named "Shamu."

An unamused "Shamu" took the photograph, tore it up, and placed it with the discards. "I have to split this with 100 other dealers," he said sarcastically.

Leonard was unfazed.

Britney's baggage

For years I've lampooned Britney Spears for her lame tipping. She either never understood or didn't care about the concept of taking care of people who do the grunt work. When she checked out of the Aladdin, now Planet Hollywood Resort, during a January 2006 visit, it was clear her handlers had read a blurb I ran about her stinginess a few days earlier.

After Spears' two SUVs were loaded with a ton of bags, one of her handlers pulled out two $20 bills, then made a show of holding them aloft so everyone could see them before passing them along to the bag handlers.

Not so lucky was the driver who spent four hours chauffering Spears around town without getting so much as an "Oops, I did it again."

Bolton bolts

No one was singing, "That's What Love is All About" after singer Michael Bolton, his drummer, and his bodyguard played a round of golf at Lake Las Vegas' South Shore country club before his lakeside concert there in August 2005. They apparently forgot proper golf etiquette: No one tipped the cart boys, the beverage cart gal, or the assistant club pro who accompanied them.

No dough from T.O.

Dallas Cowboys wide receiver Terrell Owens and his party not only didn't tip, they walked away from a $200 limo tab over New Year's weekend 2006. His rep, Kim

Eldredge, emailed me confirmation that Owens took a limo with friends early on January 1 from Caesars Palace to the Palms. "A less than five-minute ride," she said. Five minutes? On New Year's weekend?

A Fast buck

Sports broadcaster Brent Musberger left a dollar tip for a beer at a Bellagio bar, and when the bartender momentarily turned away, he looked over to find the dollar bill — and Musberger — missing.

Say it ain't so, Joe

In better days for *Girls Gone Wild* creator Joe Francis, the video entrepreneur played up to $30,000 a hand, ordered Opus One and Cristal by the bottle, and behaved like a prima donna. Since he was equally famous for stiffing his cocktail server, the dealers, and anyone else he came in contact with, the Las Vegas service industry likely showed little sympathy for his extended jail stretches in Florida and northern Nevada when hard times fell upon him.

Dishonorable mentions

Speaking of dogs, Atlanta Falcons quarterback Michael Vick walked off without tipping after buying a round for his posse at The Venetian's center bar. This was about the time the Feds were investigating his dog-fighting ring, so maybe he was conserving cash for his legal defense.

Philadelphia Eagles quarterback Donovan McNabb took a hike at Treasures strip club one day, leaving a measly $20 tip after getting a lot of special attention during his four-hour stay.

And NASCAR driver Tony Stewart, after winning several thousands at a Stratosphere craps table, left a $13 tip.

The whale of whales

One million dollars was merely tip money to Kerry Packer, the Australian media mogul whose December 2005 death was mourned on Las Vegas Boulevard.

"He regularly tipped Bellagio dealers $1 million. All 700 dealers would get a cut," MGM Mirage Resorts' President Bobby Baldwin told me. I asked Baldwin to separate fact from fiction when it came to some of the Packer stories.

No. 1: "The Texan"

Packer was at one table, and the Texan playing one table over wanted some bigger action. He asked Packer if he could join the table. Packer turned him down. "The other guy said, 'I'm a big player, too. I'm worth $100 million.'

"Kerry said, 'If you really want to gamble, I'll flip you for it (the $100 million).'"

The Texan quietly went back to his game.

"True," said Baldwin.

No. 2: "The mortgage"

Packer appreciated the service an MGM Grand cocktail server was providing. He asked her if she had a mortgage. She did, and he said, "Bring it in tomorrow and I'll pay it off for you."

"True," said Baldwin. "It was for $150,000."

No. 3: Betting $200,000 per hand?

Also true. "He was a legendary character," Baldwin said. "He dwarfed the other guys (noted whales such as Sultan of

Below: "Packer" Australian for big tipper.
Photo: Rob Griffith/AP

Brunei and Adnan Khashoggi, the arms dealer). Kerry played higher and he played for 40 years."

Good day for dealers

The dealers at Caesars Palace had a particularly good day in November 2007 when a high roller left a $250,000 tip. Tips are shared, so this was not the day to have phoned in sick.

Wouldn't Jack Bauer have a tip calculator?

Kiefer Sutherland, who plays agent Jack Bauer in the TV hit *24*, won over some servers and Bunny dealers at The Playboy Club in 2007. He had a $20,000 comp and ran up a bill of only $250. After leaving a $300 tip, he later asked the Bunny server, "Did I leave enough?"

Worthy of knighthood

Bring up Sir Charles Barkley's name and the reaction is always the same: Prince of a guy, big tipper. "I probably made $7,000 or $8,000 in one year because of Charles Barkley alone," one dealer told me. "When he'd hit a number on roulette, he'd always throw in a $500 chip, and he did that all day and all night, win or lose, no matter how big the stack."

Mr. Generosity

Funnyman Drew Carey, now the host of *The Price is Right*, frequently dropped $5,000 tips on the dealers at the Hard Rock Hotel after some hot runs. But that was chump change compared to what he left in Las Vegas strip joints. "The girls would see him come in and they'd start dreaming about a new car," said a Vegas insider who was familiar with Carey's generosity.

Andre the Giant (tipper)

Andre Agassi gave the dealers something to talk about at the opening of Red Rock Resort in April 2006. The

Las Vegas tennis great bought $10,000 worth of chips and quickly turned it into $15,000 before pushing it all back to the dealers.

King of the C-notes
Boxing champ Floyd Mayweather, Jr. routinely lays $100 tips on nightclub employees, "even when he's not drinking." One night all 40 employees at OPM at the Forum Shops at Caesars (now Poetry) got C-notes from Mayweather and the door register walked with a $500 toke.

The "rain" man
Nobody made it "rain" in Las Vegas strip clubs like Dennis Rodman. For more than a decade, he'd walk into clubs and casinos with a garbage bag full of bills of various denominations and let 'em fly.

Sharing the wealth
Cirque du Soleil founder Guy Laliberte plays big and tips big. Spies tell me he won well over $500,000 in 30 minutes at The Mansion, the MGM Grand's palatial hideaway for high rollers. "He's a platinum player, the highest level, and an awesome tipper," says a spy.

Giving 110 percent
Harrison Ford won over some new fans in the service industry during a Las Vegas visit. He was spotted at the downscale Wild Wild West casino, having breakfast at 5:30 a.m. with two "trucker types." On his way out, Ford left a $29 tip on a $20-something tab.

Our favorite low roller story
After her November 2006 concert at the MGM Grand Garden arena, where tickets went for up to $1,000 each,

Barbra Streisand was spotted playing blackjack for a miserly $15 a hand in the hotel's enclave, The Mansion, with her pet poodle seated at the table. Her dog was seen drinking from a china saucer at the blackjack table.

If you think this might be some cause of embarrassment for the super-diva, think again. Streisand returned a year later to the weekend to sing — not for long and hoarsely with a cold — to a private VIP crowd gathered for the christening of Planet Hollywood. She announced to the entire audience, "I doubled my money the last time I was here. I took a hundred and made it two hundred. Dollars, that is. But I was very happy."

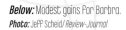

Below: Modest gains for Barbra.
Photo: Jeff Scheid/ *Review-Journal*

CHAPTER 3 – Celebrities Behaving Badly

Sometimes James Gandolfini can't escape his character. He was channeling his Tony Soprano alter ego during a dust-up at Pure nightclub inside Caesars Palace after the *Earth to America* benefit concert in November 2005. After arriving with a group of friends, he retreated to his room for a couple of hours before returning to rejoin his goombahs.

Gandolfini became irate when he learned his party had been moved from their area to make room for a group of hotel executives. What Gandolfini didn't know was that a member of his party f-bombed the execs' point man while waving a threatening finger in his face. That got Tony's boys (none of them cast members) tossed. When Gandolfini returned, he went off on security. And all that after his group had been treated to five bottles of Dom Perignon at $700 a bottle.

By comparison, actor Tom Hanks came into the same wrap party and made a point of introducing his wife, Rita Wilson, to the security crew. *Seinfeld* co-creator Larry David went up on the terrace and told jokes to security for an hour and funnyman Dave Chappelle treated the packed main room to a 3 a.m. riff of his classic, "I'm Rick James, bitch!"

Above: Where does Tony Soprano end and James Gandolfini begin?
Photo: Courtesy HBO

Below: Oommpah! Chelios' had a big fat plate breaking party.
Photo: © Dave O. of North Vancouver, Canada.

Culture crash

Hockey great Chris Chelios got an icy reaction one night at a Las Vegas restaurant.

A captain of the scandal-scarred 1998 U.S. Olympic hockey team, Chelios pushed his luck when he started dropping plates at FIX, a popular Bellagio restaurant.

He was escorted out of FIX during a 2004 dinner outing with a group of celebrities who were in town for Hollywood producer Jerry Bruckheimer's annual Bad Boys Invitational Hockey Tournament weekend.

Chelios told management that his bad table manners were "OK, because I'm Greek," referring to the Greek tradition of breaking plates.

After cooler heads prevailed, Chelios was allowed to return to rejoin his pals, who included tennis star Jennifer Capriati, Cuba Gooding Jr., Alan Thicke, and NHL colleagues Sergei Fedorov, Luc Robitaille, and Marty McSorley.

The 1998 U.S. Olympic hockey team came under heavy criticism when their Olympic Village rooms were damaged following a stunning quarterfinal loss at Nagano, Japan. The team's coach, Ron Wilson, called for the players responsible to come forward and acknowledge their "deplorable act." Team Captain Chelios was later exonerated by the NHL.

Chelios had acted out before in Las Vegas. A couple of years earlier, while in town for a radio promotion, he went to Morton's steakhouse for dinner with some station executives. He got up from the table, went to the lobster tank and picked out a beauty.

Only problem was, instead of having it prepared, Chelios reached in the tank, retrieved the lobster and took it back to the table, where he slathered it with butter and whacked it a couple times with a knife before management intervened.

No angel

Criss Angel was living the Las Vegas dream.

Standing on the Luxor stage that soon would be transformed into his $100 million magic show, he reflected on what seemed like a mirage in the desert: "About 12 years ago I came to Las Vegas," he told a press conference crowd in March 2007. "I had no money. I slept in a hotel right down the block. I rented the cheapest car I could rent. I used to drive up and down the street and look at a Siegfried & Roy billboard and just fantasize and dream about one day ascertaining (we think he meant "attaining") the kind of success that I could only imagine."

Driving down Las Vegas Boulevard now was a whole different experience. Instead of low-budget wheels and lodging, he was driving a brand new Lamborghini and living atop the Luxor in a mega-suite reserved for high rollers.

This was no illusion.

Angel had reached dizzying heights in Las Vegas without ever having performed in a ticketed show on the Strip. The press conference was to announce a 10-year partnership with Cirque du Soleil and MGM Mirage, two of the biggest entertainment brands in the world.

No previous Cirque show had been built around a solo headliner. It was heady stuff for the former New York City illusionist who had earlier won the biggest gamble of his life:

Below: Angel emotes for Joan Rivers impersonator, Frank Marino at the Miss USA pageant.
Photo: Courtesy Frank Marino

"I took my mother's house, refinanced it, and did the show in Times Square right after 9/11." The show was the first with the title *Mindfreak*, and ran for more than 600 performances in the 150-seat World Underground Theater.

As his TV exposure grew, so did Angel's reputation as the new-generation magic man. Soon he set his sights on Las Vegas, where he caught some important eyes after his A&E cable series *Mindfreak* debuted to strong ratings. But near the end of that press conference, Angel went down another road that suggested his bosses might be in for a bumpy ride.

As I wrote the next day:

"Criss Angel's inappropriate language no doubt had his corporate partners rolling their eyeballs at Thursday's news conference announcing his new magic show at the Luxor. In a too-long speech, Angel elevated the discomfort level by dropping an F-bomb during an I-told-you-so rant against critics and doubters.

"After thanking his mom, brothers, late father, and God, he closed by saying, 'I want to thank all those who never believed in me, who shut the door in my face, who said I would never make it. That gave me the strength to say, you know what — and excuse the French — but you're (expletive) wrong.'"

Sure he was a little rough around the edges, but he had just been coronated The Next Big Thing and those doors that were once closing were now swinging wide open.

Right: Angel's bevy of beauties.
Photo: Cara Roberts

They were heady times for Angel and he quickly became a club-hopping fixture among the sightings in my column.

Soon he was a serial celebrity dater, with his name linked to many of Hollywood's hottest names.

His chick streak started with a sighting of Angel and Minnie Driver at Tryst nightclub at Wynn Las Vegas in late August 2006. Around Halloween, he showed up in photos with his arms around Paris Hilton's waist as she humped a stripper pole at Jet nightclub at The Mirage. In May 2007, he arrived at Jet nightclub in the wee hours and waltzed off with Cameron Diaz, shortly after meeting her at the *VH1 Rock Honors* show.

They were everywhere together, it seemed, sighted here and there, for a week or two. One week into June, Angel went public with their relationship minutes before a stunt in Times Square, where he escaped from an elevated box full of wet concrete: "This is dedicated to my new girl. You know who you are. I'll be thinking of you."

Below: Angel's celebrity friends included Minnie Driver and Cameron Diaz seen here.
Photo: © Tony Shek

When he survived the stunt, he stood with his hand on his heart and told the crowd: "I'd like to dedicate this escape to my girl 'Trouble.' I love you, baby. Have a safe trip to Europe for your *Shrek* tour."

Three weeks later, a bombshell.

On July 1, I led my column with: "Criss Angel's next big trick? Making a messy divorce disappear."

Angel, whose real name is Christopher Sarantakos, was in Nassau County divorce court for proceedings by Joanne Sarantakos of Long Island, New York. She accused him of mental cruelty and abandonment during their five-year marriage.

His marriage was news to many of his fans and most of the Las Vegas media, given his gallivanting ways.

New York's *Newsday* quoted the lawyer for Angel's estranged wife as saying the star of *Mindfreak* had been under surveillance in Las Vegas for six months and that some damaging material had been collected.

Her attorney told *Newsday* that he would subpoena Diaz the next time she showed up in New York and ask about gifts Angel might have given her.

It was a PR nightmare for Diaz, who was being branded a home-wrecker and threatened with a summons to testify. She moved quickly, disavowing the romance. Her publicist, Brad Caferelli, told *US Magazine*.com that Angel and Diaz only saw each other four times, and that the relationship was over.

Angel didn't appear to be grieving. Two weeks after his divorce-court appearance, he joined Lindsay Lohan's birthday party at Pure on the night the fresh-out-of-rehab actress showed up wearing an alcohol-monitoring device on her ankle. Lohan and her party were seen piling into Angel's black Rolls Royce Phantom after closing Pure. They reportedly made a trip to his Luxor suite. Later that day, on her way to the airport, Lohan made a side trip to the Luxor to say hello to the magic man.

A month later, Angel had the paparazzi working overtime with his late-night hotel "meetings" with an unraveling Britney Spears, who was trying to get her act together to pull off a career comeback at the *MTV Video Music Awards*. Angel was reportedly working on an illusion for her MTV appearance, but for whatever reason — some blamed Spears' decided lack of a work ethic — the illusion wasn't part of the starlet's infamously listless performance. When her comeback attempt went off the rails, Angel wisely went underground.

But he was back in the news again in December, photographed with his arm draped over Pamela Anderson, who had married someone else two months earlier. A spy who was standing nearby later told me, "Check out her body language. She was not happy about how 'cozy' it appeared."

A few days later, I ran an item quoting a source as saying Anderson had issued a directive to management at the new Company American Bistro: If Angel showed up, she and then-hubby Rick Salomon would leave. Apparently Salomon was not among Angel's fans. Shortly after that, word surfaced that Anderson had served Salomon with divorce papers on December 28.

Faster than you can say 'abracadabra,' Angel had a new lady in his life: Miss Nevada USA 2008, Veronica Grabowski, a veteran on the Texas pageant circuit.

He had a new girl and a new look; he was sporting a full black beard in mid-February when he received the 2008 Merlin Award for "Magician of The Year" from the International Magicians Society in a ceremony at the Luxor. (The society, by the way, is largely the effort of one man, Tony Hassini, and not to be confused with the more democratic International Brotherhood of Magicians.)

In early March, celebrity blogger Robin Leach reported, "This is getting really serious, folks; he even took her parents out with them for the night to see The Beatles' *Love* musical by Cirque du Soleil at The Mirage."

Given Angel's track record of hit-and-run relationships, some of us were more cynical.

Sure enough, with his girlfriend in seclusion the weekend before the Miss USA pageant in Las Vegas, Angel was spotted dancing and what was characterized as getting "cozy" with Pamela at the Elton John show at Caesars Palace.

Below: Angel with then-girlfriend Miss Nevada USA 2008, Veronica Grabowski.
Photo: Adam Chen/Pure Management Group

Over the next couple of days, sightings poured in of Angel at the Miss USA pageant.

The juiciest story of the week came out of the blue: Angel's girlfriend was flashing pricey-looking diamond earrings to fellow contestants. Angel had showed up during a break in rehearsals and, according to buzz around the pageant, he was smoothing over things with Grabowski after embarrassing her with his outing with Anderson.

The earrings matched a big honking diamond Angel had recently presented to the raven-haired Texas beauty. She was wearing it on the ring finger of her left hand, usually reserved for wedding and engagement rings.

"They're not engaged," Angel's publicist, Steve Flynn, told me that afternoon. (Angel and Grabowski broke up shortly after the pageant and she told KWWN AM 1100 that "everything" I wrote about them was wrong, specifically that she got all the jewelry shortly before the pageant. I checked back with my pageant spies; they said that's not how she portrayed it to the contestants.)

Tacked onto my account of Angel's visit with Grabowski was some late-breaking news:

"Earlier in the evening, Angel may have stepped over the line during a chance encounter with a pageant judge. While Angel was chatting with Mike Mecca, CEO of Planet Hollywood Resort, in the valet area, Mecca's wife, Sandy, joined them.

During the conversation, Angel said to Sandy Mecca, "I hear you are a judge. I hope you are going to give my girl high marks."

Sandy Mecca, during a telephone interview with me late Thursday, said she was immediately uncomfortable, "even though my judging responsibility had ended Sunday," the second day of preliminaries.

She recognized the conflict, she said, and requested that she and her husband part company with Angel.

The morning that came out in the *Review-Journal*, I headed over to Donald Trump's ribbon-cutting ceremony for the opening of his 64-story tower in Las Vegas. When the champagne toasts and congratulatory comments were over, Trump, whom I had met on his previous visits to Las Vegas, made eye contact with me and pointed to the stage steps, mouthing, "Do you want to talk?"

I nodded and made my way over to the side of the stage. He had made a point of mentioning during the ceremony that he had the tallest hotel in town. I wanted to hear more about that.

But Trump was being pulled in several directions when he descended the stairs and I decided to get two questions in quickly: Was he going to go ahead with the second tower? No, he said, not until the economy picked up. Was he aware that a pageant judge had been approached by a local headliner whose girlfriend was a contestant?

"Yes," said Trump. "We're going to have to look at that. That's not good. We don't like that."

In the newspaper business, that's known as a "follow story," and I needed one badly because the two-hour pageant would be starting about the time my column was supposed to be turned in.

The show went quickly and without incident, at least from where we were sitting.

By the time Cara and I got out of the theater and up to the mezzanine, where the VIP party was being held, it was about 8:15 p.m. I had no indication that all hell was about to break loose. Cara, however, told me later she noticed Angel with his back to us, talking to Planet Hollywood Resort public relations executive Amy Sadowsky, about 20 or so feet to our left.

As we walked toward the entrance of the VIP event, the first hint that anything was amiss came when I heard the sound of several people running. Probably some kids, I recall thinking. I was preoccupied, chatting with Sadowsky's assistant, Andrea Roqueni, who was escorting us to the entrance.

Suddenly I sensed the presence of someone rushing up to me. As I turned my head to the left, the obscenities started flying from Angel's mouth as he rushed me and my girlfriend, with his brothers, a bodyguard, and publicist in hot pursuit.

"You fuckin' idiot!" he screamed, his face inches away.

He was just warming up. The F-bombs were flying left and right. "You are a fuckin' idiot, do you understand that? You don't get anything right. It's A & E, you fuckin' idiot, not Bravo!"

I'll give him points for misdirection. He was referring to my mistaken column reference that had his *Mindfreak* show airing on the wrong cable network. Of course, that wasn't the real reason behind the blowup.

Angel was having a bad night. Little did I know how bad.

He wasn't just pissed that his inappropriate remarks to a pageant judge had appeared in the papers. His meltdown reached critical mass during the pageant broadcast when his girlfriend didn't make the top 15. When an NBC cameraman moved in to get a reaction of him in his seat, Angel flipped him the bird.

He was so out of control, I learned days later, that he walked down the aisle toward the stage during a commercial break. Frustrated with Grabowski's stage placement as the evening wear walk-through was about to begin (all the contestants were allowed to participate), he let go with a couple of profanities while hollering and signaling for Grabowski to switch places with another contestant.

During our altercation, his entourage restrained him as he continued to run his mouth, while poking a finger toward my face. "You will never fuckin' talk to me ever again! Never!"

"I'll try to get over it," I said, knowing immediately it probably wasn't the smartest thing to say.

Incensed, Angel broke away and came charging back towards me. His fast-thinking publicist Steve Flynn jumped in between us as Angel continued to rant.

As his posse again led him away, he had a parting shot.

"Don't write another word about me, or you'll need an eye-patch over your other eye," he cracked.

"Good one," I replied. "Never heard that one before."

I've heard a lifetime of one-eyed jokes since losing vision in my right eye at age three when the suspenders on my pants came loose and blinded me. I tolerated the jokes in my youth, after having the eye removed when I was 10. At 65, I was decades past the point of letting someone get away with a cheap shot. Especially a 40-year-old headliner-to-be who should know better.

Meanwhile, Roqueni was tugging at me, doing her best to get my attention and get Cara and me safely into the party.

My Coors Light had just arrived when I saw Angel walk into the party area and head toward Mike Mecca, president and CEO of Planet Hollywood Resort. For the next 15 minutes, Angel gestured wildly, no doubt explaining how I had wronged him.

My account of the incident appeared in the Sunday edition of the *Review-Journal*. It was written as straight-forward as the thousands of AP stories I had filed over the years.

"Illusionist Criss Angel, the star of the *Mindfreak* reality show, freaked out Friday after his girlfriend, Miss Nevada USA 2008, Veronica Grabowski, didn't make the finals of the Miss USA pageant.

Shortly after Grabowski was eliminated, Angel was seen flashing a middle finger during an NBC telecast when a roving cameraman attempted a celebrity-in-the-crowd shot at Planet Hollywood Resort's main theater."

By the time you read this, *Believe* should be open at the Luxor, and time will tell whether Angel's antics were merely a punk-rock approach to publicity, or if he really does lack the coping skills to anchor a high-pressure production.

I watched NBC's flop of a reality/talent show, *Phenomenon*, when Angel, in the role of a judge, tried to hijack the show's entire concept. He blew up at one of the contestants, mentalist Jim Callahan, challenging the claim that he could communicate with the dead. And he taunted the show's star, Uri Geller, daring him to prove his mind-reading capabilities.

Upon his return to Las Vegas, Angel told Alicia Jacobs, entertainment reporter at KVBC-TV, Channel 3, that he was feeling emotional and vulnerable over the loss of his father (in 1998) and was offended that Callahan was "exploiting it for money." Had security not intervened, Callahan "probably would be in a hospital right now," Angel said.

Two months after the altercation at the Miss USA pageant, Angel showed up at Blush Boutique Nightclub at Wynn Las Vegas with a black eye.

The explanation from Flynn was that Angel got too close to a Brahma bull during a video shoot for his Cirque show, and came away with a shiner.

I should have sent him an eye-patch.

Butt head

John Lennon flirted with a serious butt-kicking during a visit to the Playboy mansion west.

The incident occurred during the Beatle's boozy year-plus separation from Yoko Ono, when he was in Southern California to get his stuff together. Lennon showed up at the Playboy Club and "misbehaved a little bit, and a couple of my friends took exception to it," Hugh Hefner told me in an interview at the Palms during the weekend of his 81st birthday celebration.

"I didn't witness it. I was elsewhere in the mansion. He put a cigarette out on a Matisse (painting), and one of my friends was gonna. . . . " Hefner said, without finishing.

"But he had been drinking. I was a huge fan. He was under a tremendous amount of pressure, very inappropriate pressure, you know, from the government. It was strange times."

Blown assignment

American Idol contestant Kimberly Caldwell was involved in a Hard Rock Hotel bar fight while in Las Vegas as an on-air reporter for TV Guide.

Caldwell, then 22, was unable to make it to an *American Idol* audition because of the altercation in the Body English club. She was a contestant in the 2003 *Idol* competition, making it to the top seven.

Flight risk

American Idol judge Paula Abdul rarely offers a discouraging word on camera, but came off more like Simon while pitching a fit after a New Year's weekend outing in Las Vegas.

PBX operator Carol Good and night auditor Damon Rosa lost their jobs at the Silverton casino after Abdul strolled in at dawn on January 2, 2006, and requested they change her airline connections. Minutes after returning to the hotel, she called at 6 a.m. for a 7:40 a.m. flight, a nearly impossible request in this age of long security lines. And remember, this was New Year's weekend.

Good and Rosa were suspended and later fired after Abdul couldn't get on the flight.

After I reported their firing, Silverton president Craig Cavileer issued a statement saying that the allegations were "totally unfair to Ms. Abdul, as she is recognized as one of the most kind, compassionate and caring personalities in the world."

In his statement, Cavileer said the Silverton felt it was "necessary to clarify that the alleged decision to recently terminate two of our team members was not based on any request or direction of Ms. Abdul as has been reported by the media."

"He's full of it," said Good. "My termination paper says 'rudeness to customer' and Damon's says 'did not provide customer service.'"

Good said she was leaving work at the end of her overnight shift that morning when Rosa asked if she could check some flights for Abdul, who had called shortly before 6 a.m.

With Rosa overwhelmed by guests checking out, Good

Below: Paula Abdul made Simon Cowell look like the nice judge during one trip to Sin City.
Photo: Cara Roberts

pitched in and was preparing to call Abdul with the information when the former recording star called and "went off on me."

Eye witness

Almost a year before the Silverton episode, Abdul was safely on the sidelines when an Oscar party catfight broke out in 2005.

Abdul, who was working the Oscars as a correspondent for *Entertainment Tonight,* was a couple of feet away when an altercation erupted between two young ladies.

Abdul reported that the girls were fighting over George Maloof, owner of the Palms Hotel & Casino. Maloof confirmed by voicemail that a "little scrap" had occurred but he declined to go into details.

The combatants included a Playboy Playmate and a future Bunny dealer at the Palms' Playboy club who made it to the cover of the magazine.

Apology accepted

Paris and Nicky Hilton, after a loud and stormy exit from Pure nightclub on New Year's Eve of 2005, returned the next night to apologize. They were upset that Paris' 20-year old boyfriend Stavros Niarchos was not allowed to enter the club.

A model of professionalism

Seattle Mariners slugger Bret Boone had an interesting explanation after acting up at Wynn Las Vegas in 2005. After a bartender requested that Boone remove his feet from a bar stool, Boone went bonkers.

"The bartender comes over and it's not, 'Mr. Boone, please,' it's 'Get your (bleeping) feet off the chair.' Yeah, I should have put my feet down, but don't come at me aggressively. Be a professional about it."

Britney Spears: Vegas was a bad influence

Britney Spears is known worldwide as a distraction from war and serious news, but Las Vegas enjoys a special place in her ongoing tabloid saga.

In my first eight years at this job, no one created a greater Vegas celebrity buzz; each visit brought new controversy. Spears got married on a whim and showed us many times over how cheap she could be (and I mean that more ways than one). She lip-synced in concerts. Fed her Chihuahua on the bar at the upscale N9NE Steakhouse. Partied with Paris. Drank and went tannin' while pregnant.

She invented new ways to stumble, personally and professionally.

My first Britney-is-clueless item appeared in late 1999, during the week of the Billboard Music Awards.

In a city where stiffs (bad tippers) are reviled, Brit, then 18, got off on the wrong foot. She showed up with friends for lunch at Gordon Biersch Brewing Company — a freestanding restaurant east of the Strip in the Hughes Center office park — and ordered a latte. Her server apologized, saying the restaurant didn't have lattes, but volunteered to dash to a nearby Starbucks and grab one. "Great," said Britney.

At the end of lunch, the server merrily informed Brit that management had picked up the check. With that, away they went. Without leaving a tip. Which not only stiffed the server, but cost her money out of her own pocket as a reward for the coffee sprint.

The next time Britney registered on our Vegas radar was in April 2003, when she surfaced at the Palms pool, sunbathing in a teeny red bikini. Later that night, she and Palms owner George Maloof were seen having drinks at the House of Blues Foundation Room, the semi-private club atop Mandalay Bay.

With that friendship forged, Spears and Maloof teamed up in a publicity plot. That September, she returned to the Palms for a "surprise" three-song concert inside Rain nightclub. It had the makings of a marriage made in heaven: the red-hot pop princess and Maloof's hip and happening Palms.

But when Britney returned with family and friends for a long New Year's weekend, Maloof — who had a long-running crush on Spears — couldn't have imagined

Above: Chillin' with Paris Hilton.
Photo: Review-Journal archives

the storm that was about to put the Palms on the world map, far surpassing even the boost he got from an infamous season of *The Real World* based there a year before.

On New Year's Eve, a Thursday, I was standing on the chilly observation deck of the ghostbar, waiting among a capacity crowd for the $500,000 fireworks display along the Strip. My girlfriend leaned over and said, "Britney's dancing right behind you."

Sure enough, there was Spears, dancing on the glass inset, a cigarette in hand. The next time I turned back, she was gone.

She had gone to Maloof, I learned a few days later, to complain that a certain eye-patched columnist was on deck.

At that point, if I were that image-conscious, I would have made sure I didn't do something really stupid. Like, say, get married at 4 a.m. in Las Vegas. But that's what happened two nights later, when she and childhood friend Jason Allen Alexander got hitched in the wee hours of January 3 at The Little White Wedding Chapel on the Strip.

Below: Spears poses with a fan.
Photo : Cara Roberts

That was surprising enough, but the bigger shock was that the annulment was in motion by afternoon. When it was over 55 hours later, Spears' publicist called it a case of two young people who "took a joke too far."

A case could be made that it was more than a first cry for help; it was the defining moment that the train started careening off the rails. In an interview days later with Katie Couric on *The Today Show*, I suggested the quickie marriage was "more about Justin than Jason."

The unraveling was underway and every visit to Vegas, it seemed, added momentum to her spectacular fall from grace.

With a divorce from Kevin Federline in the works in November 2006, Spears came to Las Vegas to do some studio work on a new album. But she made more headlines club-hopping for the first time with Paris Hilton. In yet another move that suggested an addiction to attention, she doffed her black pants to dance in fishnet stockings barely covered by a white shirt.

Her bad-mommy reputation on the rise (her two children were born in 2005 and 2006), Britney hoped to prove she could steer clear of controversy during her appearance as the countdown host of New Year's Eve 2006 at Pure Nightclub at Caesars Palace, a gig that paid a reported $200,000 just for showing up and chatting up the right people.

Instead, it was another image disaster when she had to be assisted out of the club before 1 a.m. after having too much of something.

Two months later, after a string of bizarre outings in Los Angeles, she shaved her head and wound up in rehab. She returned to Las Vegas in late March, on a very low-profile trip that reportedly involved the latest in liposuction technology as talk of a comeback grew.

All summer long, rumors flew that she was going to launch her comeback bid, after a four-year hiatus, at the Palms on September's *MTV Video Music Awards.*

When she arrived several days before one of the biggest events of her career, the reaction was "S.O.B." — Same Ol' Britney. She cut loose on the nightclub scene and let her rehearsals slide. After a backstage drama hours before she was to open the show — her hair stylist quit when she insisted on going brown instead of blonde — Spears took her first steps toward a comeback.

But the limp, lip-synced performance of "Gimme More" became another national punchline. Within days, Live Nation, the world's largest producer of concerts, killed a pending multimillion, 30-market tour deal, an insider told me.

Britney had far bigger concerns by early 2008, when her life spiraled out of control. She was held in a hospital for psychiatric evaluation and her father, James Spears, was put in charge of the troubled pop star's welfare.

Above: Father of the year and bon vivant Kevin Federline.
Photo: ©Hot Rod Homepage-Geoffrey Chandler

Hubby of the Year

No wonder Britney Spears unraveled.

Hours before Spears flew in on a Sunday night in 2005 to attend *O* at Bellagio with her then-husband Kevin Federline, he was spotted getting lap dances at the Spearmint Rhino topless club.

Rodman's crash test

Former NBA star Dennis Rodman had a painful introduction to a light pole in the parking lot of a Las Vegas strip club.

Rodman crashed a borrowed motorcycle about 9 a.m. outside the topless Treasures in October 2003. The incident killed his NBA comeback (a $10,000-a-game deal with the Denver Nuggets) and left him with 70 stitches, Rodman wrote in his book, *I Should Be Dead By Now.*

As Rodman was being transported through University Medical Center, a cop followed "toting my D.U.I." While at the hospital, Rodman said he convinced the policeman he had not been drinking — when, in fact, he had been on a several-day bender, he wrote.

New arena for Tyson

Mike Tyson put on a bizarre marathon show one night on the go-go stage at OPM inside the Forum Shops at Caesars.

Tyson "borrowed" about two dozen bar towels to hand out as souvenirs. He'd towel off the sweat and toss the keepsakes into the crowd of female spectators. As he was leaving the club, a group of female fans hoisted him overhead as they descended the stairs. His mood took a quick turn, however, when Tyson became enraged

and threatened to pulverize three guys before security intervened. Then he grabbed a female tourist who was snapping some photos, and the slurring ex-champ invoked his four favorite words, which began with "Show me your. . . . "

Above: And in this corner... Mike Tyson.
Photo: John Gurzinski/*Review-Journal*

Pricey pillow talk

Paris Hilton's then-beau Stavros Niarchos had to put more than $25,000 on a credit card after a pillow fight in his buddies' room made a mess at the Hard Rock Hotel following Kelly Osbourne's birthday bash in November 2005.

A broken sprinkler head caused water to seep into several rooms below. Witnesses said wet feathers covered the scene of the crime and Niarchos was seen shirtless with white feathers in his long hair.

Though a Niarchos bodyguard told Hard Rock supervisors, "Why are you upset? It's all going to be paid for," a spy said the young heir had to call his dad for approval on the credit card charge.

Stuffy diva

Madonna expressed herself loud and clear before agreeing to sing two concerts in Las Vegas in May 2006. She ordered the air conditioning to be turned off at the MGM Grand Garden Arena before her shows.

That explained why it was "ridiculously hot" said Riviera drag star Frank Marino, who attended one of the shows. She made the same demands at her after-party. She had Tao club management seal the air vents with tape before she arrived. Then, with the lounge closed off to the general public, she hosted a party with 150 members of her *Confessions* tour. Granted, air conditioning is a concern in the entertainment business; voice problems can cost performers millions in lost revenue. But who really cares how well Madonna sings?

Pamela's potty mouth

Pamela Anderson's mouth is not always pretty.

As she was preparing to walk a red carpet at Tryst nightclub at Wynn Las Vegas in October 2007, her wrangler was overheard asking her if she wanted to talk to the media gathered for Richard Branson's charity poker tournament.

"They can suck a dick," sniffed the star.

Anna Nicole Smith: The party never stopped

The queen of hard living, Anna Nicole Smith only added to her train wreck of a reputation during her final visits to Las Vegas.

Her most-publicized appearance came two years before her death, when she was hired by Planet Hollywood founder Robert Earl to host the 2004 New Year's Eve countdown at a high-roller event. The timing couldn't have been better for Earl, who was converting the Aladdin Hotel to the Planet Hollywood resort and looking for a publicity splash.

But the party happened to fall the day after a California appeals court reversed her $88 million inheritance award in the case involving her late billionaire husband, J. Howard Marshall. Smith had met Marshall in a Houston strip club in 1991, when she was 23 and he was 86. They were married 14 months before he died.

When Anna Nicole learned that her beloved had not provided for her in his estate planning, she sued. She was awarded $474 million, only to see it reduced to $88 million. That was reversed 24 hours before she got to Las Vegas, and she was ready to pop her cork when I caught up to her after the midnight countdown.

I waited until she had finished taking a photo with a short, pudgy VIP before approaching. She was flirtatious and more than a little tipsy when I introduced myself. Before I could ask her about the court reversal, she insisted on a photo, perhaps thinking I was part of the photo op line. When I brought up the court setback, the sweet Anna Nicole immediately turned cold.

"Those judges were so paid off!" she said.

I knew I had struck gold with that quote, and with her attorney, Howard K. Stern, standing nearby, I decided to double down. Her response was going to be big news, and it needed a comment from Stern.

Not surprisingly, he went ballistic: "Don't print that! You can't print that!"

I figured he was going to keep badgering me to not run it, so I decided to leave.

Before I got to the door, the photographer who took our photo approached me and gave me his card. It was her private photographer, Larry Birkhead — who was, of course, much later revealed to be the father of the baby she left behind.

The next day I got a call from Aladdin illusionist Steve Wyrick, who had a hot story he wanted to share.

Anna Nicole had attended his show, along with Stern, Birkhead, her son, Daniel, and dog Sugar Pie. He invited her to the stage for a levitation.

Anna Nicole liked something about Wyrick — maybe his Texas drawl — and she had a performance of her own in mind. Wyrick wouldn't go into the details, but he made it clear something happened backstage, and not just some playful Texas grab-ass. A few months after her death, Wyrick told a tabloid publication the initial encounter involved an oral levitation performed by Smith, followed by a rough sex encounter in her hotel suite.

By the way, Birkhead emailed me five weeks before Smith's death, asking if I would mention that he was seen partying with Pamela Anderson at Tao, The Venetian hotspot, on New Year's Eve 2006.

By doing him a favor, I was adding a connected name to my source list. I took advantage of the opportunity to get an update on his lawsuit against her, claiming he was the father. A Los Angeles Superior Court judge had just ruled that DNA testing had to be done by January 23. "My birthday's the 22nd, and it's going to be a good day," he said by telephone.

Little did I know that a struggling photographer who was requesting a self-sighting would soon be a member of the lucky sperm donor club, and a multimillionaire.

(This reminds me of one of my most-used lines when people ask me how they can get their name in the column. I usually stop 'em in their tracks when I say "For $500, I'll put you in. For $5,000 I'll keep you out, so behave." One night, after getting a laugh with the line in front of a local women's organization, an attractive lady approached me with a big smile, reached out and put something in my hand. When I looked down, it was $500 in cash and her business card. I handed the money back to her and explained to her that it was just a joke.)

Anna Nicole hadn't registered all that much on the Las Vegas radar prior to her 2002 reality show hit, *The Anna Nicole Show*. She had appeared on *Penn & Teller's Sin City Spectacular,* a weekly cable show that ran for a season on FX in 1998. It took the reality show to make her star power as undeniable as a highway crash you slow down to see. While shooting scenes for it, she stayed in a high-roller suite at the Rio and shot an episode with the male dance troupe Chippendales. Spies told me she made no secret of her interest in luring several members of the Chippendales back to her boudoir. But after several attempts at 4 a.m. booty calls, she got no takers and called it a night.

In September 2005, Anna Nicole spent six hours at

Below: Escapade with magician Steve Wyrick gives magician's assistant a whole new meaning. Photo: Courtesy Steve Wyrick

Sapphire Gentlemen's Club, tipping big for lap dances from her favorite female dancers. She rode to the club in a limo bus equipped with a stripper pole. When the bus stopped at stoplights, pedestrians crowded around cheering as Smith, 80 pounds lighter from the diet pills she promoted, gyrated on the pole.

But my all-time favorite Anna Nicole story came from salon operator Michael Boychuck, better known as Paris Hilton's personal "blonder."

In the 1990s, Boychuck was working in Jose Eber's salon on Rodeo Drive in Beverly Hills. One day, word came that a spokesmodel for Guess — the name didn't register with Boychuck — was coming in for a blonde treatment. Minutes after settling into the chair, a fidgety Smith told Boychuck and stylist Laurent, "I hope you don't mind, but I'm burning up."

The sun-burned Playmate then stood up and disrobed.

All she was wearing was her birthday suit.

Boychuck's job: apply the moisturizer.

Left: Smith attended Planet Hollywood's grand opening.
Photo: Denise Truscello/Courtesy Planet Hollywood,

CHAPTER 4 – Class Acts

You won't find any demanding divas or sorta-celebs in this chapter.

Be thankful all celebrities don't come from the just-spell-my-name-right generation. We raise a toast to those who take the time to share their talents or make a statement through deeds and decency.

Meet Miley Cyrus

Miley Cyrus took the time to make a surprise visit to the children's cancer ward at Sunrise Hospital during her January 2008 concert stop. The 15-year-old star of *Hannah Montana*, Disney's runaway TV hit, stunned a room full of kids when she walked into their play area during her 90-minute visit.

Below: Miley with Tamara Matthews at Sunrise Hospital. *Photo:* Courtesy Monique Matthews

"They were really surprised," said Monique Matthews, whose daughter, 12-year-old Tamera, was among the lucky ones who not only met Cyrus, but got to attend one of her three concerts at the MGM Grand Garden arena. "She lifted spirits," Matthews said. "It's so nice to see famous people help the kids."

"She's really sweet," said Tamera, who needed a boost after eight months in the ward. "Some kids were too sick so she went to see them."

Cyrus' visit made a difficult weekend more bearable for Tamera's mother. "I found out Saturday that she has relapsed," said Matthews, who also learned that same day that Tamera had been invited to the concert. Tamera wasn't told about her setback until after the visit.

"I didn't want to say anything until afterward," said the mother of three. When Tamera heard the prognosis from her mother, "She told me, 'At least I got to meet Hannah Montana.'" Matthews lost her battle with cancer a few months later.

Above: Liza Minelli brought back the "gypsy show."
Photo: Stephen Chernin/AP

Liza loves Las Vegas

Liza Minnelli revived a Las Vegas tradition with an '80s-era flashback performance during a 2006 engagement at the Luxor.

A month earlier, during an interview on the Luxor theater's stage, I asked her to name her most memorable Vegas show.

"I loved it when Sammy (Davis) and I did a special show at two in the morning after we had both done (our own) shows. We did a special show for entertainers. It was at the Riviera, and it was sensational."

She never forgot how much it meant to the rank-and-file entertainers who usually were working in their own revues while she was performing.

As a matter of fact, she told me she was going to dinner that evening with Luxor and MGM Mirage executives and planned to propose such a "gypsy show" when she returned a month later for her Thanksgiving weekend engagement. A couple of days later came the announcement that the gypsy show was on. The result was the most electric crowd reaction of my Vegas years.

"With 23 standing ovations," I wrote, "and too many affectionate shout-outs to count, more than 1,000 showbiz kids and headliners showered the Broadway and film icon with appreciation during her two-hour show in the Luxor Theatre."

Keep in mind that it didn't start until after 1 a.m., when many a crowd would be dozing off and a 60-year-old legend would be winding down.

The singular moment of a momentous night came late in the show when Minnelli called time out.

"Wait a minute," she said. "I can't see a damn thing," as she plucked off her iconic eyelashes.

You never heard such a roar.

Family treasure

When live auction bidding for two racquets offered by her husband Andre Agassi roared passed $300,000, Steffi Graf returned to the stage of Agassi's annual Grand Slam for Children benefit and bought them back for $360,000.

Graf said the racquets belonged in their home. One was the racquet used during his first pro win in 1985; the other was the one he played with in his U.S. Open finale in September 2006.

Below: Las Vegas' favorite son Andre Agassi and wife Steffi Graf at the Planet Hollywood grand opening.
Photo: Tom Donoghue/Courtesy Planet Hollywood.

Above: Gracious Ben Vereen.
Photo: Cara Roberts

Bouquets to Ben

Song and dance icon Ben Vereen made a big impression at the 2007 premiere of *Monty Python's Spamalot* at Wynn Las Vegas.

And it had nothing to do with his fashion choice for the night: an all-black Victorian-era outfit, complete with a cape and top hat.

As my girlfriend and I were chatting with him near the front of the stage while waiting for the crowd to thin out, he leaned over the edge of the orchestra pit and told the orchestra, "Thank you, ladies and gentlemen."

It was a gesture as thoughtful as when he showed up at a Las Vegas hospital to visit the deathbed of 91-year-old legendary choreographer Henry LeTang. Vereen was one of LeTang's biggest admirers, and showed up unannounced to wish him well.

Vereen lifted LeTang's spirits by breaking into a tap dance. "The nurses went gaga," said Arlene LeTang, Henry's daughter-in-law.

Hal Lubarsky's amazing story

Hal Lubarsky made history in the 2007 World Series of Poker as the first blind player to cash in the main event.

In one of the more remarkable stories in the event's almost 40-year history, Lubarsky finished in the top 200 of the 2007 main event, outlasting more than 6,000 players, to win $51,000.

When he busted out of the tournament, play stopped long enough for the remaining players and a large crowd to give Lubarsky, 46, a standing ovation.

Lubarsky's accomplishment was achieved with the help of two card readers, which was an issue at first because players are not supposed to be aided. But Lubarsky raised the ante for tournament organizers when he suggested he might sue, claiming discrimination against the blind.

The readers, one of them a Las Vegas bartender, would whisper the hole cards to Lubarsky, an elite cash player before his sight faded. "The dealer then announces the flop," explained WSOP spokesman Nolan Dalla. "He (Lubarsky) had to assimilate all the information. It's one of the most amazing stories we've ever had."

Lubarsky suffers from retinitis pigmentosa, the same genetic disorder that slowly robbed much of the vision of casino mogul Steve Wynn. "It's like looking through a straw," he told MSNBC.com.

His vision loss started accelerating in 1998, at age thirty-seven. "A lot of people treated me bad because I would slow down the game because I couldn't see well. I was like an outcast to a lot of people who didn't like losing to me."

Unable to see clubs and spades and needing assistance

Above: Amazing poker player Hal Lubarsky.
Photo: Joy K. Miller/IMPDI

Prince requested Pure's VIP Red Room be cleared so he and his gal pal could have privacy at the Caesars Palace nightclub.

Presumably he shared: Prince ordered 40 shots of Patron tequila and a veggie burger one night at Tao (Venetian) in 2007.

Still mysterious after all of these years, Prince left 'em guessing after dedicating "Purple Rain" to someone "I promised to play this for" during his club opening show at the Rio in November 2006. There was speculation that the tribute was to CBS newsman Ed Bradley, who died of cancer a couple of days earlier. Bradley had interviewed Prince on *60 Minutes*.

Right: Prince performed at Tiger Woods' charity concert Tiger Jam. *Photo:* KM Cannon/ *Review-Journal*

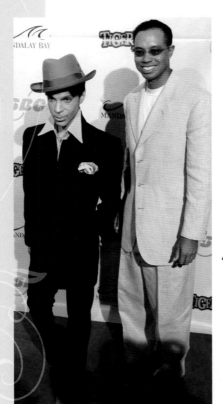

from the dealer in identifying the overturned cards, he quit playing live games about three years ago. He kept his skills sharp through online play and when he returned to the poker rooms, he recruited friends to sit behind him and whisper his cards.

"I can see probably ten percent, but I can't see people at all if the lighting is low. In my own house I still walk into stuff. I can't see cards at all."

He can read his handwriting as long as he writes in large letters with a black felt-tipped marker.

One of Lubarsky's heroes is casino mogul Wynn, and not just because they share the same rare condition. A few years ago, Lubarsky wrote a letter to Wynn, asking for a favor. "I asked him if he would hire my wife, who is a dealer," said Lubarsky.

A couple of days of later, the phone rang at the Lubarsky home. The man on the phone identified himself as "Wynn Resorts" and asked Lubarsky's wife, Jan, if she could go to work immediately. She quickly agreeed.

"She was the last dealer hired, and we're sure he helped," said Lubarsky.

In fact, a betting man would wager it was Wynn on the phone.

Smokey's the best

In an age when too many celebrities expect a free lunch, Motown great Smokey Robinson is a breath of fresh air.

During a 2006 dinner outing off-Strip at Lotus of Siam, Robinson not only sang some of his hits to a restaurant full of diners, but on the way out, he picked up the tab of about $3,000 for the entire eatery and left a $500 tip.

A man of substance

Before Al Jarreau's show at the Sun Coast in November 2005, Lisa Boyens, one of his long-time fans, sent him a bouquet of roses. Late in the show, Boyens told her husband, Craig, that she was feeling tingling and numbness in her hands and face.

While leaving the showroom, she collapsed and went into a coma after suffering a brain embolism. She was rushed to Desert Springs Hospital.

Boyens' family, including her four children aged three to 14, received a much-needed boost two days later when the Grammy award-winning jazz musician arrived with a rose from the bouquet she had given him.

Boyens, 39, died two days later. Family friend Randy Walker said Jarreau's gesture "was such an amazing sign of support for someone so busy to go to the hospital and take the time to get the children's names before he arrived. He told them he would dry out the flowers and give them to the family."

Below: Check please! Smokey Robinson treated surprised diners.
Photo: Marian Umhoefer/ *Review-Journal*

Above: Al Jarreau paid a special visit to a dying fan.
Photo: ⓒ Jasper De Boer

Above: Tarantino, seen here with Fergie, celebrate their mutual birthdays.
Photo: Courtesy Ana Dobrijevic

A man of generosity

Hollywood writer-director Quentin Tarantino, who gave us gore galore in *Reservoir Dogs* and *Pulp Fiction*, showed off his grindhouse tastes during a 2005 Las Vegas visit. He was spotted at Club Paradise with 15 female employees he took on an all-expenses paid trip. That must have been one kill(er) bill.

The other Rosie

Rosie O'Donnell isn't all sound and fury. During a dinner at N9NE Steakhouse at the Palms, she sent a bottle of Dom Perignon to a newly engaged couple.

McCartney's first impression

Paul McCartney loved, loved *Love*.

"He said, 'I wish there was more time between acts so that we could applaud the cast,'" Mirage president Scott Sibella said of the star's reaction to the Beatles-themed Cirque du Soleil show. "He was singing along, clapping his hands. He said it was beautiful, inspiring. He said he loved it."

McCartney came away from his first viewing ten days before the 2006 premiere in an ecstatic mood. After the show, he went backstage to meet the cast and crew. He told Michael Moloi of Johannesburg, South Africa, the boot stomping dancer in the "Lady Madonna" segment, "You'll have to teach me that."

Cool Clooney

Opposite page: All you need is love. Celebrities come out for the opening of Cirque du Soleil's *Love*.
Photo: Isaac Brekken/ *Review-Journal*

George Clooney made a lot of fans backstage at The Mirage after he caught Cirque Du Soleil's *Love* in August 2006. Instead of immediately meeting with the artists as most celebrities do, Clooney took the time to stop and thank the crew first.

Family man

Cirque du Soleil creator Guy Laliberte gave his family a lot of love during the week of the gala opening of *Love.*

The French-Canadian billionaire flew in 75 family members for the June 2006 premiere and the 50th anniversary celebration of his parents, Gaston and Blandine Laliberte. They renewed their vows at a Bellagio wedding chapel before having dinner at Julian Serrano's Picasso restaurant.

"I am what I am from them. This is my gift to them," said Laliberte, a former street busker.

What a catch

Former NFL running back Robert Smith scored some points during his January 2006 bachelor party at the Palms when he wore a football jersey with the No. 1 on the front and "Jennifer" across the back.

Above: Clinton granted a presidential pardon to nervous food server.
Photo: ©Roger H. Goun

Presidential pardon

Former President Bill Clinton, who knows a lot about forgiveness, went to bat for a nervous server. During his 2005 Halloween weekend visit to N9NE Steakhouse at the Palms, Clinton had a tray of food, including chicken and mashed potatoes, spilled on his lap. As the visibly shaken server cleaned up, Clinton leaned over to Palms owner George Maloof and said, "Please don't fire him."

Great save

When Las Vegas gastroenterologist Dr. Julian Lopez watched the 2005 World Series from the owners' box at

U.S. Cellular Field in Chicago, it was a payback for an act of kindness. Long-time Chicago White Sox co-owner Eddie Einhorn credits Lopez with saving his life.

Einhorn, the Sox' longtime vice chairman, told the *Chicago Sun-Times* he was in Las Vegas for a Sox spring training game when he was beset with stomach troubles. During his trip to the hospital, Einhorn met Lopez in the emergency room. Lopez informed Einhorn he had acute pancreatitis. They stayed in touch, and through a chance occurrence, Einhorn's mother went to Lopez's office seeking a doctor.

Before long, Lopez was the Einhorn's family's physician, and when the White Sox moved their spring training camp to Tucson, Arizona, Lopez's son served as a batboy.

Above: Going above and beyond the Hippocratic oath.
Photo: Martin S. Fuentes/ *Review-Journal*

After the pancreatitis scare, Einhorn's condition took a turn for the worse when he went in for a follow-up diagnostic procedure. "I was in a coma for 28 days. I almost died," Einhorn told the *Sun-Times'* Carol Slezak. He made it through that, too.

But his health took another downturn in 2005. Einhorn was getting ready to go on dialysis when Lopez told him by telephone, "I want to give you a kidney. I got an extra one and you need one."

"The day I decided to become a doctor is the day I made a solemn commitment to spending my time trying to make a difference in other people's lives," says Lopez.

Celine Dion: Giving back

Celine Dion put the diva question to rest quickly.

Soon after arriving in Las Vegas in 2003, she was spotted pushing a piled-high grocery cart through a Wal-Mart late one night in suburban Henderson.

A three-year deal with Caesars Palace that could be worth $100 million and she's running her own errands?

So much for "Diva Las Vegas."

What did we expect from such entertainment royalty? Well, the earliest rumors got her future neighbors riled up, after I reported she would be taking a helicopter to work from her waterfront property in Lake Las Vegas. The issue blew up, and at the May 2002 press conference formalizing the Colosseum run, the singer was asked point-blank if she planned to catch a chopper to Caesars. Her answer was a guarded, "Sometimes."

But when Rene Angelil, her husband/manager, emphatically told me later there was nothing to the rumor, I gave him the benefit of the doubt because he always had been a straight-shooter with me.

The week before the launch of *A New Day* we saw the important side of Celine.

The father of 17-year-old Stephanie Richardson called me several days before the show was to open. His daughter, a student at Eldorado High School, was only a few days away from dying of cancer. Jim Richardson wondered if there was any chance Celine could reach out to his daughter, whose last wish was to meet her.

I ran a column item and contact with the Richardson

Opposite page: Creative director Franco Dragone with Celine Dion at her Vegas farewell in December 2007.
Photo: Jane Kalinowsky/*Review-Journal*

family soon followed. Taking time out of an impossibly busy week of rehearsals and last-minute details, Celine called Stephanie and spoke to her by speaker phone just hours before the teen passed away.

A year and a half later, I interviewed Celine backstage and asked her about desperate requests from families like Stephanie Richardson and those who seek comfort in her music. Many came to her for a few words of solace, she said, with their stories of losing loved ones.

An older couple brought a keepsake of their personal loss. They had lost two sons in the September 11, 2001, attack on the World Trade Center in New York. One son was a New York firefighter, the other a New York police officer. The parents wanted her to have a badge that belonged to one of them. Another woman was still traumatized from seeing one of the hijacked 9-11 jets fly into the tower.

Often, with the show two minutes away, Celine said she was on the telephone offering words of hope to the dying because, "I have this gift." Others have died while she was holding their hand. "I heard their last breath," she said, choking up. "I feel very fortunate. I feel like I'm escorting them to heaven."

During the final week of *A New Day* in December 2007, the singer apologized to the crowd. "The show started so late. If it starts on time, then we get it over with quicker. And it's not good, so that's why we were late tonight." She chose not to bring down the crowd with the real truth: The show started late because she was meeting with terminally ill children from the Make-A-Wish Foundation.

We heard plenty about Celine, the doting hands-on mom. For Halloween in 2003, she and her husband joined Rene Charles, four months shy of age three, for an evening of trick or treating. Rene Charles' costume? An Elvis outfit, complete with a microphone, of course.

Two weeks after the Halloween sighting, an aspiring songwriter called me and asked if I could help him grab Celine's attention. John Henderson, a 53-year-old chemical engineer, told me he had forked over $1,000 to run the following message on a billboard and bus stop bench: "Celine Dion, I've written a song for you, please call for words and music. John Henderson (XXX)-2145."

"You've got to take chances. If you don't, you'll always regret it," said Henderson, who had the signs put up along a street Celine would take on her limo rides to work. (Lucky for John that the helicopter never came to pass.)

Three weeks later, I got a call from Henderson, who was over the moon with joy. Not only did he gain an audience with Celine, but he was booked on ABC's *Jimmy Kimmel Live*, where he would sing the love song he pitched to her.

Henderson added that when he played the CD backstage to Celine and Angelil, she began harmonizing along to his song. "She told me twice that I have a fabulous voice . . . very powerful and dynamic. Rene said they won't be recording for another year, but he said 'I'll promise to consider it for the next album.' They were so good to me."

In March 2005, there was a most un-Celine-like sighting: the Canadian songbird stood out like stilettos in a bowling alley when she showed up at the NASCAR event at Las Vegas Motor Speedway. She was there for the kid. Rene Charles, barely four years old, had developed a raging case of NASCARitis.

Angelil explained: "For Christmas we gave him some little cars. He knows all the car numbers and the drivers,

Above: Celine made time to hear a fan's original song.
Photo: KM Cannon/ *Review-Journal*

and he loves Tony Stewart." Stewart put his young fan behind the wheel and gave him a number of souvenirs, including a signed replica of the orange No. 20 Home Depot Chevrolet.

"This is a great, great day for him," said the happy father.

In an entertainment era dominated by diva behavior, Dion was one of the least controversial Las Vegas headliners of her stature. Nonetheless, she could not evade the scrutiny of the *Fox News'* Bill O'Reilly when she criticized the slow response to victims of Hurricane Katrina and President Bush's Iraq policy.

The post-hurricane aid delays were "not acceptable," she told CNN's Larry King. New Orleans police should have been rescuing survivors instead of arresting looters, added the singer, who, along with her partners in *A New Day*, donated $1 million to the hurricane relief effort.

"That's just dopey," said O'Reilly. Looters are dangerous, he added. "You don't excuse anarchy." A tearful Dion questioned Bush's decision to go to war in Iraq: "How come it's so easy to send planes in another country to kill everyone in a second, to destroy lives?"

A few weeks later, she told my *Review-Journal* colleague Mike Weatherford that the outburst on CNN was "a buildup inside of me like a volcano. I could see the rage inside of me as a mom, as a citizen, as a human being, and couldn't see the changes as fast as I wanted. I couldn't take the pain and couldn't take the images every night and every morning . . . I just couldn't hold it anymore and I just exploded."

"It's not often that I open up and talk this way. Maybe that's why it made an impact," she added. Later, she teamed up with Elton John and Jerry Seinfeld on her Caesars stage in a benefit for Harrah's Entertainment employees affected by the hurricane.

It wasn't the first cause she stood behind. Moved by the needs of Opportunity Village, a local charity for the intellectually disabled, Dion and Angelil agreed to donate all ticket sales from an Easter Sunday performance to the organization. "She's very passionate about people with disabilities," said Linda Smith, chief development officer for Opportunity Village.

On a cold December 28, 2003, the Angelil family visited the organization's annual Magical Forest attraction. "She was here for two-and-a-half hours," Smith says. And when it was time to go, "she welled up with tears when we thanked her. It was very moving for all of us shivering outside."

It was a far cry from the carpetbagger scenario predicted by an unnamed Las Vegas headliner, who told *Newsweek* Dion would come to town and "suck up all the oxygen and then fly away."

But when the singer wrapped *A New Day* and quickly embarked on a year-plus world tour, she said Las Vegas is now "a little bit my hometown and I'll tell you why: I've never lived in another place for five years. Even Florida, I don't even know if I lived there that long."

"When I'm back in the area," she added, "It's going to be like singing to my hometown."

CHAPTER 5 – Infamous Meltdowns

There's no shortage of competition for the category of Sin City's most glaring human train wreck.

Topping a lot of lists would be Shecky Greene's high-speed car crash into the fountains at Caesars Palace in the late 1960s. Sam Kinison would get a lot of votes for the night he tried to go on stage at Bally's after an all-day binge in the '80s.

Or the night a snockered Frank Sinatra kept reading the cue cards at a celebrity roast at the MGM Grand in the '70s, unaware he had gone through them once.

Moving up fast on all of them, Britney Spears.

The Hoff hits bottom

Nothing says, "I've got a drinking problem" like eating a burger off the carpet.

David Hasselhoff's memorable crash-and-burn moment ended up on YouTube, where millions saw the jaw-dropping video. Performing in *The Producers* at Paris Las Vegas, a shirtless Hasselhoff was filmed in a stupor, eating a hamburger while sprawled on the floor of his hotel suite. His teenage daughter Taylor Ann, who shot the video, can be heard saying, "Tell me you are going to stop. Tell me you are going to stop."

Shortly before the video sur-

Opposite page: The Palms Casino Resort showed its support during Paris' incarceration. *Photo:* Courtesy Palms Casino Resort

Below: Would you like fries with that? The Hoff's infamous video of him eating a hamburger on the floor was shot in Vegas. *Photo:* Cara Roberts

Palms carpet photo: David G. Schwartz

Opposite page: Live From Las Vegas, the Juice Show. O.J. Simpson faced kidnapping charges from incident at Palace Station.
Photo: Gary Thompson/ *Review-Journal*

faced, I was tipped that Hasselhoff had missed a show. I sent an email to Hasselhoff's publicist, Judy Katz, to check on his status. Her response: "David did not do the show last night or the matinee today. He had some kind of stomach thing going on. Apparently he and Joe, his driver, stopped and had some fast food yesterday afternoon that didn't agree with either one of them."

Hasselhoff's affection for fast food was evident in the video when he appeared to have more interest in a giant hamburger than assuring his daughter he would stay clean and sober. When the video surfaced, Hasselhoff's handlers told the media his daughter filmed him drunk so he could later see how awful he acted. The tape revealed that Hasselhoff's daughter was concerned he was going to be tested: "You're going to be fired from the show."

While she pleads for him to stop drinking, he is heard f-bombing her.

Another attempt at spin came when the media were told the video was shot three months before. After the video went public, Hasselhoff, who often showed up in the nightclub sightings in my column, released a statement saying he was a recovering alcoholic.

Cirque du O.J.

NFL Hall of Famer O.J. Simpson brought a new show to town in September 2007. Cirque du O.J. was equal parts freak show and media circus.

Simpson's trip to Las Vegas for a friend's wedding turned into another appearance behind bars, after he and some comrades invaded a hotel room in what he called a "sting" operation to recover some of his sports memorabilia from a vendor.

He was charged with almost a dozen criminal offenses, including first-degree kidnapping.

The Heisman Trophy winner was arrested after a col-

lector reported a group of men burst into his room at the Palace Station casino and, after at least one weapon was allegedly brandished, made off with several items Simpson claimed belonged to him.

Simpson's biggest mistake? Accompanying his posse into the room and confronting two longtime collectors of his memorabilia.

Three days later he was arrested and jailed, creating an unprecedented media frenzy in Las Vegas reminiscent of his murder trial in Los Angeles. On the day of the hearing, the scene outside the Clark County Court House looked like central casting for a B movie.

Above: Carlin refused to tone down his act.
Photo: Ralph Fountain/ Review-Journal

Carlin's Flaming Finale

The late comedian George Carlin ended a four-year relationship with the MGM Grand in not-so-grand style. No subject was sacred the night Carlin finished his December 2004 run at the hotel. He riffed on suicides and beheadings and, near the end, made it clear he couldn't wait to get out of "this fucking hotel" and Las Vegas.

He told the crowd of 700 that he was looking forward to going back East, "where the real people are." He added, "People who go to Las Vegas, you've got to question their fucking intellect to start with. Traveling hundreds and thousands of miles to essentially give your money to a large corporation is kind of fucking moronic. That's what I'm always getting here, these kind of fucking people with very limited intellects."

When a female in the audience hollered something that sounded like, "Stop degrading us," Carlin fired back.

"Thank you very much, whatever that was. I hope it was positive. If not, well blow me."

Carlin was iconic through and through. He moved to the less prestigious Stardust rather than heed MGM requests to tone down his act. "I would feel like somebody's pawn, like they get to run my art and they don't," he later explained to the *Review-Journal*'s Mike Weatherford. And he offered a near-apology for ripping into the audience: "You don't get hard-core fans every night filling every seat. You get that on the road. In Las Vegas, the audiences are mixed, because that's the nature of the city."

Before he returned to the Strip four months later, however, Carlin checked himself into rehab to break a "Vicodin and wine" dependency. In April, he came back sounding more mellow about Vegas. He blamed his frustrations on being fired for being, "Too dark." Carlin died in June of 2008, a week after performing at the Orleans.

The Albrecht incident

Chris Albrecht, chairman and CEO of Time Warner's HBO cable network, had his career crash hours after watching Oscar De La Hoya and Floyd Mayweather, Jr., fight on May 5, 2007.

His arrest for assaulting his girlfriend at 3 a.m. in the MGM Grand's valet parking lot led to his resignation four days later.

A recovering alcoholic, Albrecht, 54, had been celebrating the richest fight in boxing history, a $120 million haul from HBO's pay-per-view telecast. He was seen tossing down tequila shots at one of HBO's post-fight parties.

In a memo to staffers before entering rehab, Albrecht wrote he'd been "a sober member of Alcoholics Anony-

Above: HBO CEO's career knocked out after assault of his girlfriend.
Photo: Las Vegas Police Department

mous for thirteen years," until two years earlier, when "I decided that I could handle drinking again. Clearly I was wrong. Given that truth, I have committed myself to sobriety."

The incident came at the apex of his 22-year career at HBO, after he built the cable network into a powerhouse on the strength of such hits as *The Sopranos*, *Sex and the City*, and *Six Feet Under*.

Fame game

Things got a little sketchy about 3 a.m. one night at Art Bar, one of the newer downtown-revival hangouts.

The crowd noticed something different right away about the three guys who walked in and headed for the pool tables.

"One looks like a Jimmy Page impersonator, one's pretty nondescript (but in a hip way!), and the last looks like a member of Sergeant Pepper's Lonely Hearts Club Band," bartender Matt Sorvillo recalled in a blog. "Sergeant Pepper" was wearing a dark green, plush woman's overcoat, complete with broach, wrote Sorvillo.

While Sorvillo was waiting for someone in the party to approach the bar, his female boss struck up a conversation. Sorvillo noticed the nondescript member of the trio was now at the bar, "when the baby-faced one, dressed like Dame Edna, hollers 'Hey, you mind serving my friend?' in a not-so-polite way."

Long story short, Sorvillo asked for identification upon serving three beers, and "'Sergeant Pepper' ignores me and walks away. I repeat myself. He says he's not drinking."

Sorvillo sticks to his guns. He served three beers; he needs three IDs.

'Sergeant Pepper' says, "C'mon," adding he didn't mean to be a male body part, "but you were ignoring my friend."

Above: You got to pay to play, or at least have valid ID. Rock group The Killers made a scene at the Art Bar.
Photo: KM Cannon/ Review-Journal

No, said Sorvillo, he wasn't ignoring anyone, he was talking to his boss, and he still needed IDs.

"Finally, Sergeant Pep admits he doesn't (have an ID). The beers go back on ice and I tell them they have to go. Being a sailor (aboard a Yellow Submarine) and not willing to take any shit from a lowly barkeep, Pepper does what any self-respecting military man would do. He complains to my boss," using X-rated language.

The trio "got pouty . . . grumbled, huffed and puffed, and stormed out the door. And in one final act of rebellion, 'Jimmy Page' knocked all the fliers next to the door off the shelf, and all over the floor."

Sorvillo's boss, a smallish woman, chased the trio to their SUV in the parking lot, yelling for them not to come back, he wrote. When Sorvillo went back behind the bar, a regular leaned in and asked, "Do you realize who those guy were?"

"Those were The Killers," said the patron, referring to the Las Vegas-based group that had recently hit the big time. Sorvillo told me that he went online, "pulled up their pictures, and it was them."

They had stopped in several times, said Art Bar co-owner Jesse Garon. "Tell 'em to come on back, and we'll give all the free draft they want, but please bring the licenses."

The Godfather goes gonzo

The late James Brown went off the rails during his last Las Vegas performance, a New Year's Eve show to ring in 2001 at the short-lived Blue Note club near the Aladdin (now Planet Hollywood).

First, he walked on stage in a bathrobe and started jawing with early arrivals, who had no clue what was going on. Then he threw a chair at a table of ladies who were minding their own business. Later, he told the audience he had communicated with the Pope and it was come-to-Jesus time.

The next day, The Godfather was spotted outside the Blue Note at noon, dashing into the street in his underwear and ranting at motorists.

Chapter 6 – Best Quotes

You know a city has reached epic proportions when "Vegas" and "God" show up in the same sentence. "Las Vegas is sort of like how God would do it if he had money," said hotel and casino developer Steve Wynn, whose vision revitalized the city's sagging image in the 1980s.

Opposite page: Wynn Resort & Casino cuts a distinctive profile. *Photo:* David Vasquez *Inset:* Hotel and casino developer Steve Wynn changed the Vegas skyline. *Photo:* Duane Prokop/ *Review-Journal*

Ray Romano's Las Vegas shtick includes this classic spin on the city's now-iconic slogan: "What happens in Vegas stays in Vegas, but the rash doesn't."

Some of my other favorites:

Mouse Fears

Hours before the Wynn Las Vegas premiere of *Monty Python's Spamalot*, which happened to be on his 64th birthday, I asked creator Eric Idle what the Pythonite recalled about life in England during World War II. I got more than I bargained for.

Below: Eric Idle dances with John O'Hurley at the *Monty Python's Spamalot* debut party. *Photo:* Cara Roberts

Idle said he recalled "the bombings, more particularly, the air raid sirens. I had a Mickey Mouse gas mask, which has given me a lifelong fear of Disneyland and rubber, and left me sexually stunted."

Roseanne dogs Tom

Roseanne Barr, during the *Comic Relief* show at Caesars Palace in November 2006: "I don't think we should hang Saddam Hussein. That's too good for the bastard. I think he should have to marry Tom Arnold."

Caan can quip

James Caan, introducing the perpetually tanned George Hamilton at the 2006 Nevada Cancer Institute benefit as "the fifth best-looking black man in America."

Dog bite

"Wayne Newton's back from Iraq, where his hair was used as body armor." — Triumph, the Insult Comic Dog (Robert Smigel), at the 2006 Comedy Festival at Caesars Palace.

Wynn's first impression

"The first time he (Steve Wynn) saw the dress rehearsal of *Mystère*, he told me, 'Franco, your show is beautiful, but it's boring like a German opera.'" — Former Cirque du Soleil director Franco Dragone, a creative force behind Cirque's early success in Las Vegas with *Mystère* and *O* at former Wynn properties.

Above: Comedian Romano presented a different spin on Vegas' slogan.
Photo: KM Cannon/ *Review-Journal*

Right: Mr. Bojangles stood-up for his friends.
Photo: ⓒAlan Light

Better than Jacko-world

Palms owner George Maloof is relieved Michael Jackson and his family failed to build a planned Jackson-family themed casino on the land where the Palms now stands.

"Neverland Casino?" mused Maloof during the E! network's *Billionaire Brotherhood*.

Don't go there

"Let me know when you stop being a legend, so we can start being friends again." — Sammy Davis, Jr. to Bobby Darin, after Darin brashly stated his goal was to "pass Frank (Sinatra) in everything he's done." — Michael Starr's *Bobby Darin: A Life*.

Tyson talk

"The knee's okay. I'm training confusciously everyday." — The malapropism-prone Mike Tyson during an interview before the Bernard Hopkins-Oscar De La Hoya fight in September 2004.

A few kind words

"She is one of the most loving and caring people I know. It's harassment and horrible, what's going on, and my love and prayers are with her and her family. She's an absolute goddess." — Jeff Beacher, creator of the Beacher's *Madhouse* comedy revue, on the jail sentence handed down to his pal Paris Hilton, who boosted the *Madhouse* with her attendance.

Above: Paris sports a $1 million poker chip dress with George Maloof at the Palms Casino Resort grand opening.

Photo: Courtesy Palms Casino Resort

Memo to Mel

At a media gathering before his annual Labor Day telethon in September 2006, 80-year-old Jerry Lewis had the perfect punishment in mind for Mel Gibson, who had made news for his anti-Semitic tirade during a traffic stop: "I am doing a film with Mel Gibson and his father. I'm going to direct it and I'm going to call it *Skinheads*, and we're going to open in Haifa and then go to Berlin and Jerusalem and Tel Aviv."

Getting the party started

"It's Hammer time!" — Rapper MC Hammer, as he escorted Motley Crue frontman (and *Surreal Life* co-star) Vince Neil down the aisle at his January 2005 wedding at the Four Seasons. Neil got hitched to Lia Gerardini.

Above: "It's Wedding Time!" M.C. Hammer helped out *Surreal Life* co-star Vince Neil during his 2005 wedding to Lia Gerardini.
Hammer photo: ⊛magerleagues/ Andrew Mager
Neil photo: Craig L. Moran/*Review-Journal*
Below: Hollywood legend Tony Curtis.
Photo: Norm Clarke

A Slappy Flashback

"The trouble with unemployment is that the minute you wake up in the morning, you're on the job." — Slappy White, the late comic sidekick to Redd Foxx, who lived in Las Vegas and had his initials placed on the chimney of his home.

Harvey's hello

"Greetings from the miracle in the desert, the vaudeville of the sand dunes, the mother of all strip malls — Las Vegas." — Broadway icon Harvey Fierstein's opening line in a guest column for the *New York Post* while he was exiled for a run of the musical *Hairspray*.

Skin city

"That was more 'out' than 'fit'." — Las Vegas novelist Michele Jaffe, commenting on a barely-there costume at the 2004 Pimp 'n Ho Ball at the Orleans.

Sizing up the crowd

Film legend Tony Curtis at a 1989 party marking former mob attorney Oscar Goodman's 25 years in Las Vegas, commenting on the "colorful" characters in

the crowd: "I don't know why I'm here. I didn't kill anybody." Goodman went on to become a two-term mayor in Las Vegas and Curtis a Las Vegas resident.

Above: The world's happiest mayor attends events with showgirls in tow.
Photo: KM Cannon/ *Review-Journal*

Briefly held

After NFL lineman Ross Verba blew through most of the half-million he won at the Palms, Cleveland *Plain Dealer* columnist Chuck Yarborough observed, "(While the article) didn't say what game the ex-lineman was playing when he won his cool half mil, I have a guess, given his NFL history: Texas Hold 'em."

Roker's Food rule

"I have a rule that I never eat anything bigger than my head." — NBC weatherman Al Roker, trying the monster pancakes at Hash House a Go Go during a breakfast with Martha Stewart, after his weight loss of more than 100 pounds in early 2006.

Medical mixology

"Morphine and prune juice. A strange cocktail." — Clint Holmes, after returning to the stage at Harrah's Las Vegas less than three weeks after colon cancer surgery.

Above: "It's a good thing" - Roker enjoyed breakfast with Martha Stewart.
Photo: © NBC Universal, Inc

Right: Vegas favorite Clint Holmes is a survivor.
Photo: KM Cannon/ *Review-Journal*

Above: Miraculous recovery for Manilow.
Photo: Sara Tramiel/*Review-Journal*

Swan Song

The last song Buck Owens sang was for those who ached to find fame in Las Vegas. Owens ended his final show in March 2006 in Bakersfield, Calif. with "Big In Vegas" from the same-named album he recorded in Las Vegas in 1969. The lyrics include: "But my dreams still linger on though my hopes are almost gone/But my will is strong and I've got to make it big in Vegas."

A new man

Las Vegas Hilton headliner Barry Manilow, out of action for nine weeks after arthroscopic surgery on both hips, opened his return with "It's a Miracle" in November 2006. Then he told the crowd, "These are my fabulous new hips, Milli and Vanilli."

Pink's policy

"I'm not gonna do a Britney and pop out some kids. I'm not a Happy Meal. My husband's got the burger, but he's not getting the fries and shake to go with it." — Singer Pink, who married Las Vegas motocross star Carey Hart in January 2006. In early 2008, they announced they were splitting.

Above: Pink-The Anti-Britney!
Photo: Ruben D. Luevano/*Review-Journal*

CHAPTER 7 – Adventures on the Celebrity Trail

ver since I arrived in Las Vegas in 1999 to chronicle celebrity adventures and misadventures, there are two questions I hear most often:

Opposite page: The Strip by day.
Photo: Jon Sullivan/PD Photo

No. 1: How do you get all the tips?

It's quickly followed by, How do you know the information is true?

The short answer to No. 1: From every level of Las Vegas society. From City Hall, cabbies, cocktail servers, public relations worker bees, and bouncers to the underbelly. The Internet also made it so much easier for tipsters to contact the media.

Here's how the top ten stories I've had in Las Vegas fell in my lap:

1. Britney Spears' surprise wedding: An anonymous call to my cell phone from a Nebraska area code started it all.

2. Michael Jackson's 2006 Christmas Eve move to Las Vegas: A source at the private airport where Jackson's plane was landing.

3. First word that Britney was pregnant with her first child: It started with an unrelated call to Los Angeles. After denying it for three weeks, she confirmed.

4. Ben Affleck's big blackjack win of $660,000 at the Hard Rock Hotel in 2000: I had an anonymous tip that Affleck was there. I went to investigate, but he had already left. However, through sheer luck, I ran into a local publicist for a show on the Strip who confirmed seeing him. I made a call to a former Hard Rock employee who not only confirmed it, but added more detail; Affleck was playing three hands at a time of $20,000 each. After

his big win, he handed more than $100,000 of it back in tips to dealers and cocktails servers.

5. Australian media mogul Kerry Packer's worst gambling setback in Las Vegas — more than $20 million — came when he was forced to spend several extra days at Bellagio after planes were grounded in the wake of the September 11 terrorist attacks: an anonymous dealer provided tons of details. After I reported Packer's big loss, Bellagio president Bobby Baldwin called me and asked for a come-to-Jesus meeting in his office with *Review-Journal* publisher Sherman Frederick and me.

6. Kid Rock's early-morning raid on what he thought was Tommy Lee's suite at the Hard Rock Hotel: My source called about 15 hours before the episode with an amazingly accurate prediction of what was going to happen. I can forgive his psychic powers for failing to predict Kid would end up knocking on the door of the wrong room. (See Chapter 11 for the entire account.)

7. Julia Roberts and Catherine Zeta Jones skinny-dipping with their body doubles at 5 a.m. in the Hyatt Regency's Jacuzzi following the 2001 wrap party for *America's Sweetheart*: My source not only witnessed it, but he had brought a video camera to work days earlier in the event something might materialize that he could sell to the British tabloid newspapers. He would have won the lottery had the camera batteries not been dead when he went to film the frolicking.

8. Celine Dion's decision to become a Las Vegas headliner, major news in 2001: I got the jump on the story when a local PR lady called with news that Celine was spotted at Street of Dreams, a home show for over-the-top houses, and overheard the star say she was moving here.

9. A steamy slow dance involving Julia Roberts and George Clooney during a cast-and-crew party in the

Bellagio's Fontana Lounge during the first week of filming *Ocean's Eleven* here in 2001: Another spy on the set supplied that one. It was newsworthy because about two weeks later, it was announced that Roberts and Benjamin Bratt had split.

10. Pamela Anderson's birthday suit dance for Hugh Hefner on his 82nd birthday: When Hef walked in, she walked out of a bedroom in the Hugh Hefner Sky Villa in the Palms Fantasy Tower wearing only high heels. It was the hottest text message I ever received.

How do I know the information is accurate?

It's all about contacts, contacts, contacts. You start building a network of "spies" from the day you arrive in town, taking down telephone numbers, from valets to strippers to high-level executives. What do they get out of it? For most of them, it's the thrill of knowing they provided the inside information. When you hear a secret, aren't you usually dying to tell it to someone? And in some cases, such as Britney skipping on the tip, it's sweet, anonymous revenge.

I didn't get off to the best start in my new job in Las Vegas, after 15 years in Denver as a sportswriter, sports columnist, and man-about-town columnist. The first thing I encountered was a five-decades-old policy of Sinatra-esque silence when it came to cooperating with the new guy in town. It was nothing personal, just the way the town had operated through the tight-lipped and paranoid, mob-run years.

I sensed the general feeling in the executive chambers along the Strip was that little good could come from having one's celebrity guests mentioned in a gossip column. For one thing, it might look like the casino dropped a dime on their guests, who were dropping large bills at the gaming tables and preferred anonymity. Embarrass a VIP and (department) heads often roll in this town.

I was confident that attitude would change in time, as long as I stuck to my strength — reporting — rather than going down the snarky and salacious path. *Review-Journal* publisher Sherm Frederick always says the main thing that convinced him to give me the column was that my man-about-town writing in Denver didn't abandon the sourcing and fact-checking of my *Associated Press* days. I also had some hard-knock experience with a different type of diva, from my years in the sports world.

Back in 1978, former Cincinnati Reds pitcher Tom Seaver all but performed a wheelie on my chest after flattening me while zipping through the clubhouse. I've long been convinced it was more of a statement than an accident, considering his slow start that season after the high expectations that came with his blockbuster trade from the Mets a year before.

As far as great jobs go, my six years with the *Associated Press* in Cincinnati taught me more than any other job. Covering the Big Red Machine, one of baseball's iconic clubs, was close to the ultimate sportswriting job. There was never any confusion on my part that the *AP* wanted tough stories covered. One year you're covering a back-to-back world championship team and the next a splintered team in turmoil. I didn't go out of my way to find negative stories, but I also didn't duck a tough one.

That got me in trouble on more than one occasion. One year I was in the middle of a press box slugfest with the *Cincinnati Enquirer*'s beat writer after I ran a story chronicling the decline of the Big Red Machine. Another year Pete Rose, unhappy that I reported he had told his attorney to get him traded to Philadelphia, threatened to punch out my "fucking headlights."

He wasn't referring to my car.

So I wasn't entirely unprepared when, a mere three weeks into the new Las Vegas job, I found myself evicted from the MGM Grand, where I had just covered the Mike Tyson-Orlin Norris fight. Tyson threw a left hook after the first round ended, knocking Norris down. Norris claimed he injured his knee because Tyson tossed an off-the-clinch punch and said he was unable to continue the fight.

The fight was called and officials ruled it a "no contest." An unruly crowd was leaving when I spotted Pierce "James Bond" Brosnan walking with a security squad down a corridor near the pressroom.

Above: The MGM Grand lion.
Photo: Jon Sullivan/PD Photo

I decided to take a shot. I introduced myself and asked Brosnan for a reaction. He didn't sugarcoat it. He was disgusted with Tyson, the result, and the decline of boxing in general.

As he took off, I heard a voice coming from a security electronic device urging "everyone up to the sport book. Now!"

One of the security guards said, "They're expecting a riot because of the no-contest ruling" (meaning all bets are off and no one wins).

I joined the dash to the sports book and when I arrived, everything was calm. A fan recognized my face from my column mug shot and struck up a conversation about the fight, or lack of.

We didn't get very far into the chitchat when three security guards came up behind me, with one of them wanting to know, "Who are you and why are you asking so many questions?"

I held out the oversized credential that covered much of my chest and gave them my name and said, "I'm a reporter with the *Review-Journal* and reporters are supposed to ask questions."

"Not inside this building," came the response. "Take your questions outside, off the curb, and if you have any other questions fax them to our PR department on Monday."

They meant business and I didn't question their authority. But 30 seconds after we finished talking and I walked away, two security guards followed me and informed me I was being 86'd.

Less than a year later, I had the welcome mat withdrawn at the Hard Rock Hotel. The Hard Rock's security chief called me at the *Review-Journal* newsroom and informed me that I was no longer welcome because of my highly detailed report on Affleck's big night at the tables before he entered rehab.

It was later explained to me that it was necessary to 86 me because the Hard Rock wanted to send a signal to its celebrity clients, specifically Affleck, that the casino was not responsible for the leak. Banning a gossip columnist would demonstrate that the Hard Rock was standing by its celeb clientele.

Several months later I was summoned to the Hard Rock president's office and informed I could return, as long as I agreed not to talk to any Hard Rock employees. I politely rejected the offer, explaining that I didn't want to put an employee's job in jeopardy for simply saying hello or having an innocent conversation.

I stayed away for about a year before new president Don Marrandino reached out and thawed the chilly relationship.

It was about that same time, in late 2001, that George Maloof was preparing to open the Palms and no one could have predicted the profound effect it would have at many levels.

By embracing celebrity culture, at a time when what happened in Vegas truly stayed here (even though the slogan wasn't unveiled until early 2003), Maloof forced major properties to reevaluate their longstanding policy of not sharing much, if any, celebrity happenings. It was hit and miss, for the most part. What few sightings I received came by cultivating sources in restaurants and clubs.

Once the Palms' celebri-centric marketing plan took off, I was a major beneficiary. Maloof understood the power of celebrity news. The more celebrities who showed up, the more information that trickled in from a variety of Palms sources inside N9NE Steakhouse and ghostbar.

It wasn't long before others saw the value of getting daily mentions of their clubs and restaurants. Competitors took note, especially Light Group, Pure Management Group, and Tao. Soon the trickle became a torrent of information.

I credit Maloof for recognizing the value of allowing MTV to film *The Real World* throughout the casino. Restaurants and other public areas throughout the Palms received scads of camera time. Better still for Maloof, the young twenty-somethings thrown together in the Palm's specially tricked-up suite for the "reality" series — really more of a contrived soap opera, if you've ever watched it — turned out to be the horniest, most outrageous bunch in MTV history. *The Real World*, rerun over and over again, was instrumental in putting the Palms on the map and opened the floodgates of reality TV in Las Vegas. Before it few, if any, casinos had allowed cameras on property without absolute control of the final product.

It also didn't hurt that Matt Drudge, a fan of Las Vegas from his childhood visits with his grandmother, often returned and developed a love affair with the city.

Below: Matt Drudge witnessed Pete Rose's bitch-slap of Norm. ***Photo:*** Brian K. Diggs/AP

One day in the fall of 2003, I was having lunch with friends at Ruth's Chris Steakhouse on Paradise Road when my cell phone rang.

"Hi Norm, this is Matt Drudge. Would you go on my radio show Sunday?"

My first reaction was "I'm being Punk'd" and when I hesitated as I got up from the table to take the call, Matt took my delayed reaction as disinterest in his offer. I apologized and explained that in a city known for its impersonators, I thought a friend was pulling a fast one on me by imitating Drudge.

I was ecstatic when he mentioned he had just added "Vegas Confidential" to the *DrudgeReport.com*, the hottest website for news on the planet, with its millions of hits a day.

The first time Matt joined us for dinner, in March 2005, we took him to the hottest celebrity restaurant in town after dinner. It was a Saturday night and N9NE Steakhouse at the Palms was loud and rocking.

In my lifetime, I've never experienced a night quite like it. I'd be surprised if Matt didn't agree that it was one of the wildest dinners he's experienced.

From Matt's standpoint, it's not every day that you have dinner with two people you barely know and Pete Rose ends up bitch-slapping one of them (me) halfway through the salad course. (If you skipped the introduction to this book, now's the time to turn back for a full explanation.)

And the next thing you know, New England Patriots' quarterback Tom Brady and Palms owner George Maloof are standing at our table, and we're under the impression they just saw the whole thing.

Cara and I have since had some memorable dinners with Drudge, but nothing comes close to that Hall of Fame night. The incident definitely made an impression on Brady, because the next time I saw him he remembered me. He was slow-dancing with his then-girlfriend Bridget Moynahan in a VIP section at Tao, the hotspot at The Venetian, when he noticed Cara and me a few tables away. He whispered something to Bridget and they came over and said hello, which was either very classy or he had told her, "This is the bozo that Pete Rose smacked."

The irony is that when it comes to hits, Drudge is the king.

Five months after the Rose whacking, I came up with a delicious idea that turned into the second most-read story of my career. As Matt continued his visits, my girlfriend Cara and I became good friends with him and looked forward to our dinner outings with him. First and foremost, he's a first-rate newsman who turned a phenomenon called the Internet into one of the most powerful media outlets in American history.

Matt had everything to do with a story that trailed only the Britney Spears wedding scoop in terms of exposure.

In August 2005, during Cara's birthday dinner in SW Steakhouse at Wynn Las Vegas, I was jolted by the sight of the first $40 steak on a menu. A week or so later, I saw yet another at $40 and mentioned to Cara that I had to jump on that story. After a series of calls and a dozen or so emails, I discovered the $20 steak had gone the way of the $1.99 buffet.

The results of my research were jaw dropping. At Shintaro, the Japanese eatery at Bellagio, a 10-ounce Wagyu Kobe tenderloin was going for $190. Shintaro's 12-ounce sirloin commanded $170. Over at Bradley Ogden, the high-end eatery at Caesars Palace, the 8-ounce Kobe was listed at $175.

Also cracking the $100 barrier: a 10-ounce Kobe filet Mignon at Craftsteak inside the MGM Grand. On the cusp, a 14-ounce Kobe rib eye for $98.

My original surprise proved naive. So many steaks topped the $50 mark that we gave up on counting them.

Drudge gave my report a ride, leading the page with art of the Vegas skyline and the headline: "The Gilded Age: $200 Steaks in Vegas."

By 9 a.m., six hours after it appeared on the *Review-Journal*'s website, the site crashed for five hours. Drudge told us months later that the 9 a.m. meltdown coincided with Rush Limbaugh opening his radio show with the story. The story registered more than a half-million hits before the crash and was on pace to rival the story of Monica Lewinsky's stained blue dress.

Drudge picked up many other "Vegas Confidential" stories, which helped the column's popularity immensely and continued to fuel the rage for all things Vegas.

But the biggest story of my new career was, without a doubt, Britney's quickie wedding.

I got the tip late in the afternoon of January 3, 2004, when my cell phone rang and the Nebraska area code 402 appeared.

Nebraska?

The anonymous male caller wanted to know if I was aware that Spears and George Maloof got married. Convinced it was a prank call, I thanked the caller and said something like, "Yeah, sure, we're well aware of it." Then I put the phone down and asked my girlfriend, "Why would somebody from Nebraska be calling my cell phone with a story that Britney Spears got married to George Maloof?"

It was such a bizarre call that my gut instinct was to put in a call to Maloof.

Before he could call back, I received another call. This one came from a very reliable source, who breathlessly asked, "Did you hear the news?"

"You mean Britney Spears marrying George Maloof?" I said, assuming he was in on the joke.

"Noooooo," my source moaned. "She didn't marry Maloof. She married some guy and they're getting it annulled."

Then Maloof called, confirming that all hell had broken loose and that an annulment was indeed moving forward. I made a call to the newsroom and reporter Brian Haynes dashed over to the courthouse, quickly confirming there was indeed a marriage license issued to Britney and childhood friend Jason Allen Alexander. Our online bulletin beat the world by 45 minutes and triggered a media frenzy that I had experienced only once before, when I broke the story that Denver and Miami were being awarded National League expansion franchises. But this received major international treatment, up there with Elvis and Priscilla's surprise wedding. Or, as shockers go, Michael Jackson and Lisa Marie's.

The biggest shock was that the annulment was in motion by that afternoon. When it was over 55 hours later, Spears' publicist called it a case of two young people who "took a joke too far."

Someone's always got an agenda and it can be a challenge sorting out the tips that don't pass the smell test.

In December 2000, a club promoter insisted Madonna, amid swirling rumors that she was about to marry Guy Ritchie, was coming to the promoter's party at The Venetian. It

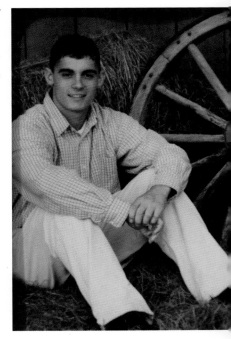

Below: Jason Alexander, Britney Spears' fifty-five hour husband.
Photo: AP Photo (high school picture)

seemed farfetched, because there was no indication she was even going to be in town for the Billboard Awards. I needed convincing and he laid it on thick, claiming he went back a long way with the superstar.

I gave in and on the day of the event, ran a line about the possibility that she would make an appearance. Not only did she not show at the party, she didn't even make it to Las Vegas. The promoter's name hasn't appeared in my column since.

More recently, a marketing director at one of the local gay clubs called in 2007 to say "Paris" was going to be at his club that night. I gave him a blurb on the website. "Paris" turned out to be a Paris impersonator. It was one of the most unethical acts I've encountered during my years here, and his word will remain worthless to me for a long time.

Regrets? Like Frank, I have a Few

One of the biggest was naming names in a marriage rumored to be on the rocks. On a very slow news day, I ran a couple-in-trouble item about country stars Sammy Kershaw and Lorrie Morgan not long after their 2001 marriage. They had no Las Vegas connection to speak of, but I went against my better judgment and ran it.

Kershaw called the next day from their home and, demonstrating far more class than I deserved, insisted it just wasn't so (the marriage lasted another six years). I was disgusted that I put myself in such a position and offered my sincerest apologies and told him I never felt worse about something I wrote.

I vowed it would be a cold day in hell before I considered doing it again.

I am often asked if I ever encounter someone who has taken offense at something I've written.

Comedy legend Jerry Lewis called me up one day and said he wanted me to stop over for a chat. I knew it wasn't likely to be a yukfest. While I sat in front of his desk, in an office that featured Dean Martin's portrait, Jerry went through a stack of negative clippings, reading them aloud.

When he got to my column, he prefaced his critique with, "Now we come to the *Las Vegas Review-Journal*, a piss-ant of a paper." He read what I wrote, which included the offending line that described him as "tantrum-throwing." He asked me if I had any idea how much that hurt his eight-year-old daughter. I got away with a minor scolding and an invitation to call him if I had a question.

Below: Legendary comic Jerry Lewis hosts his annual telethon in Vegas.
Photo: Jeff Scheid/ *Review-Journal*

I took him at his word and called him a few months later, not long after the September 11 attacks, to get his reaction to the anti-French sentiments after France refused to join the U.S. and England in taking on Al-Qaeda in Afghanistan. I knew it might be a sensitive issue with Lewis, a long-beloved comic icon in France. But I asked anyway. I recall two things: He was on his yacht in San Diego and the interview was one of the briefest of my career.

At least that was over the telephone. Comedian Robin Williams gave me both barrels in front of a crowd.

It happened on the afternoon of Andre Agassi's Grand Slam for Children benefit in October 2004, during the annual press conference in the bowels of the MGM Grand Garden Arena.

When I asked Agassi to comment on whether he had asked the performers to back off political commentary after last year — when Elton John lambasted Dennis

Miller for his Republican-leaning, pro-Bush comedy —
Williams went off on me like I was his worst heckler:
"Oh fuck off! Read the top line, man. With the good
eye, look up here. Oh back off, right. They let pirates
in. Back off, right."

The top line he was referring to on the banner behind
the dais read: "The Andre Agassi Charitable Foundation."
I'm still not sure what he meant, other than to suggest
I use the banner as an eye chart.

Ray Romano chimed in, with perfect deadpan timing,
"Does that answer your question?"

Agassi then followed: "The answer's no, however you
want to write that."

It was brutal, but that's fair, too. If you give, you
take.

Williams made a statement a couple of hours later
onstage, by delivering 37 F-bombs (yes, I counted them),
a five-minute orgasm scene with a bottle of water and
60-some other words hardly appropriate for a youth
benefit.

The annual press conference went away not long after
that, replaced by the obligatory red carpet. The comedi-
ans were a lot tamer in later years too. The only swear
word heard in 2007 — when Williams was not in the
lineup —came from producer David Foster's amazed
reaction to the quality of a performer who came up to
sing from the audience.

I may be oblivious and out of the loop, but I can
only think of one other celebrity who has made it
clear he's not a fan.

For years, I just thought Penn Jillette was
aloof. I wasn't aware there was some serious resentment until I found myself at a
large table across from him at KOI, the
Hollywood sushi emporium that opened a

branch location at the Planet Hollywood Resort.

I made about four attempts to open a conversation but nothing worked. He made it clear there wasn't going to be any chitchat and I was relieved when he excused himself from the table and left (although his wife, Emily, is a delight).

Cara picked up on the iciness and asked me about the back story.

Perhaps it had something to do with this item, which led my column on January 17, 2003:

A sacrilegious stunt by Penn & Teller that offended some at a major magicians convention was defended Thursday by fellow local headliners.

A group walked out of a roast of Amazing Johnathan on Monday after Teller, dressed as Christ on a full-sized cross, entered the room on a cart. A midget dressed as an angel performed a simulated sex act on the near-naked Teller.

Above: Magicians Penn & Teller.
Photo: Craig L. Moran/ *Review-Journal.*

Penn Jillette, in a Roman centurion costume, unveiled the scene by pulling away a "Shroud of Turin" that covered the cross.

The roast was part of the four-day World Magic Seminar at the Riviera.

Monte Carlo headliner Lance Burton, a roaster, addressed the controversy during the awards luncheon finale Wednesday that drew about 1,000.

Reached Thursday, Burton said, "I told them, 'You were warned ahead of time.' It was a roast; it was held late at night (midnight). I absolutely, positively did not apologize.

"I said, 'Penn & Teller, Siegfried & Roy, Mac King, Amazing Johnathan, and I all have different styles. That's good; that's what makes it an art form.'"

He added, "Penn & Teller are my dear friends and I would take a bullet for them. And you can write that." Amazing Johnathan said he was aware that a number of "gospel magicians" walked out and raised Cain. "This was performance art," said Johnathan. "I know that Penn is a practicing atheist, and I agree with him that Christianity can be dangerous. Look at the Trade Center. That was done in the name of religion."

The stunt drew the wrath of the largest Catholic organization in the country and readers called me to say they were going to picket or boycott the Rio. I reported on both developments.

More recently, Penn was less than thrilled again when I relayed news from San Jose in April 2006 that a radio host, John London, had been fired for offering a $5,000 reward on the air to have Jillette killed. London was incensed by Jillette's own radio show, where he called Mother Teresa a "kink" and a fraud.

Word filtered back to me that Jillette was pissed and somehow felt my reporting of the incident jeopardized his safety.

I've told you about some of the biggest stories of my Vegas years.

Let me tell you about one I missed

At the bottom of my February 23, 2001, column was this tidbit:

"One of the rarest sightings: Ex-Beatles Paul McCartney and George Harrison at Cirque du Soleil's *O* with their significant others. Backstage they chatted with performers and signed sheet music for bass player Rheal Jutras and a tambourine-like instrument for percussionist Kurt Rasmussen."

A few days later, I followed up with this additional information about the McCartney-Harrison visit: "During their backstage tour, the duo was approached by the show's clown, who sank to his knees and bowed in reverence. 'No', said McCartney, 'We should bow to you,' gesturing toward the cast and crew."

Five-and-a-half years later, I realized how badly I failed to follow up on the Beatles' visit. After a sneak preview at The Mirage of *Love*, Cirque's unprecedented collaboration with the surviving Beatles, I asked Guy Laliberte, Cirque's founder and CEO, about that backstage meeting.

Laliberte and Harrison had met in Quebec in June 2000 through a shared love of Formula One racing, and began envisioning a co-production. Ringo Starr and John Lennon's widow, Yoko Ono, approved the deal when Harrison talked McCartney into seeing *O*, Laliberte said.

McCartney had never seen one of the full-blown Cirque shows in Las Vegas, so the Harrisons and McCartneys flew in from Los Angeles. McCartney loved what he saw. But Harrison, who had been fighting cancer for some time, died in November 2001.

"When George died, I think that kind of boosted the project again, because I think everybody kind of recognized that it was the last project that George worked on and they wanted to make it happen," Laliberte said. "We thought first we'd bring the show to London, but they said no, surprisingly. They said, 'We want to do Vegas first.'"

What do you do when the telephone rings and an enraged voice demands a retraction?

It happens, and when it does, it usually means you're in for a real bad day. I had two such calls in 2007 and both

put me in an instant tailspin. Messing up the date of an event is one thing. Correcting a wrong or misspelled name is another. But when you hear "I want a retraction," there's not much wiggle room. You've probably screwed up royally.

The first case came during NBA All-Star Weekend, not exactly the time you want one of your blunders appearing in the column. The man on the telephone was Las Vegas Mayor Oscar Goodman, and he was irate.

The issue was a major story I had just posted on our new website, *NormClarke.com*. The mayor was preparing to announce a $10 billion downtown development, I was told, which would include a sports arena as the centerpiece.

"There is absolutely no truth to that and I want a retraction," Goodman claimed. "I wish it were true, but it isn't," added the mayor who had been promising a major NBA-related announcement.

During pauses in Goodman's tirade, I explained that I had every confidence in my source, but that I would check with him again and retract it if I was wrong. When I couldn't immediately reach my source, I caved. The mayor was so insistent that I pulled the item off the website and ran Goodman's emphatic denials the next day in my *Review-Journal* column.

So imagine my surprise four months later, when I opened the *Review-Journal* and read an article headlined "Another arena dream." A $9.5 billion downtown project featuring a proposed sports arena was going before the city fathers.

I put in a call to the mayor but didn't hear back on that one.

The second dispute flared up during Thanksgiving weekend, after I ran a sighting of former NBA player Walter McCarty at the Luxor's LAX nightclub with members of the University of Louisville basketball team. The item included this extra detail: Patron tequila and Clicquot champagne were the beverages of choice.

That evening I received a call from a Kenny Klein, who, in a rage, demanded a retraction. He was the school's sports information director. He insisted no team members were there and that McCarty, a former U of L star who was in his first year as an assistant coach, was by himself and most certainly was not drinking Patron and champagne.

Klein called it a "completely erroneous report" and added, "we have people crying for lawsuits." He added, "Bottom line, I know they got cameras all over those casinos and pictures don't lie. I guarantee you that there's none of our players in that casino at that time."

My response: I'll check further and get back to you.

My assistant at the time, Jeremy Pond, and I started digging, and it didn't take long to take the story to a far more serious level.

First, Jeremy looked through the local nightclub website, *NapkinNights.com,* and found a very tall athletic young man in one of the party photos. He cross-checked it with the University of Louisville media guide.

It was a match: the guy in the photo turned out to be injured Cardinals star Juan Palacios.

Meantime, I checked with some spies and learned that someone at McCarty's table purchased a $400 bottle of Patron tequila and that a bottle of Veuve Clicquot was paid for in cash. The Patron was charged to the credit card of an Eric Scott. Scott was listed as the Director of basketball operations for Louisville.

Two days after the initial item, we ran a follow story with the new information. Klein called and apologized and, I'm sure, immediately knew he had unleashed a firestorm.

Below: "Let's go to the tape." Despite denials to the contrary, University of Louisville players including Juan Palacios, left, lived it up at Luxor.
Photo: Courtesy *Napkin Nights.com*

A January 2007 sighting of Denver Broncos wide receiver Javon Walker at Tryst nightclub inside Wynn Las Vegas had all the signs of a messy retraction.

A few days earlier, Walker's teammate, Darrent Williams, died in Walker's arms during a New Year's weekend drive-by shooting in Denver. Aware of the sensitivity and the timing, I had double-checked with Wynn casino sources to be sure. But some Broncos fans weren't buying it. Several sent angry emails saying it just wasn't true, that it was a case of mistaken identity or sloppy reporting.

Below: Eva Longoria Parker and Mario Lopez.
Photo: Cara Roberts

My friends at the *Rocky Mountain News* in Denver helped me settle the mystery. Walker was "just trying to get away from Denver for a little bit" when he came to Las Vegas, team sources told the *News*. Broncos coach Mike Shanahan said Walker was unable to attend Williams' funeral in Texas because he was "devastated" and "going through some heavy grief right now."

Sometimes a hot tip arrives at a time when everyone else is reporting the opposite.

As rumors were flying that Eva Longoria of TV hit *Desperate Housewives* and Tony Parker of the San Antonio Spurs had split, one of my best MGM Grand spies came through with a sizzler in 2006. He spotted Eva riding Parker through the MGM Grand casino at 4 a.m. after leaping onto him from the front, with her legs wrapped around his waist.

One of my most exciting months in Las Vegas came when the cast of *Ocean's Eleven* arrived in April 2001 for several weeks of location filming.

I caught a big break just as the shoot was beginning. I scored a copy of the script, very possibly the only reporter to see it.

It wasn't all luck. I wanted to own that story during the movie's stay so I came up with a plan: I called the booking agents of a dozen local extras to do a story on the hometown talent and came away with cell phone numbers for almost every one of them.

A day or so later, I called one of the extras, looking for a tidbit, and got way more than I anticipated; he grabbed his script and checked on the next scheduled shoot. When he mentioned "script," I asked if I could borrow it for a few hours.

It paid off with scoop after scoop on one of the most-anticipated movies in years.

But it came at cost that I'd happily accept: Shortly after I published some of the script secrets, I was uninvited to be in a ringside scene that featured a number of local celebrities at the MGM Grand's Lennox Lewis and Wladimir Klitschko fight.

A writer's obligation to the readers should always come ahead of his desire to see what he would look like in the same movie as Julia Roberts.

But the story has a Hollywood happy ending. Six years later I made the final scene of the second sequel, *Ocean's Thirteen*, with George Clooney and

Below: Clooney at *Ocean's Thirteen* premier at the Palms.
Photo: Cara Roberts

Above: Pitt also attended the *Ocean's Thirteen* premiere.
Photo: Cara Roberts

Brad Pitt. That's me on a TV monitor as Clooney walks away during an airport scene.

Friends suggested I must have gotten back into producer Jerry Weintraub's good graces, or had something on somebody. Truth is, I had nothing to do with it. In fact, I had no idea it was going in until Carol Cling, the *Review-Journal*'s film critic, saw a screening a couple of days before the Las Vegas premiere in June 2007.

Here's how it happened: My girlfriend, Cara, is the public relations director for the Las Vegas Chamber of Commerce. About four months before the premiere, Warner Bros. contacted her and asked for copies of Las Vegas TV commercials that were unique to the city. She submitted several, including one of me in a *Review-Journal* ad, which was used in the last frames of the film.

I can't begin to tell you how surreal that was, sitting in the same theater with Clooney, Pitt, and the stars, and seeing myself on the big screen. For pulling that off, Cara deserves beaucoup evenings of dining at Joel Robuchon's and frocks galore from Betsey Johnson.

The last person on Earth I care to interview again?

That's easy: Toni "Mickey" Basil, longtime choreographer for Bette Midler.

For the 25th anniversary of her big pop hit, I set up an interview in October 2007 and asked for a telephone interview of 5-to-10 minutes. She's a local icon, having grown up in Las Vegas — she wears her Las Vegas High cheerleader's outfit in the "Mickey" video — and would soon be returning when Midler launched her show at Caesars Palace.

Fifteen seconds into the interview, she started complaining that everything I needed was on her website. It was an excruciating 10 minutes of hell, with every other question met with a whiney, "I really wish you had checked my website."

She was big-timing me and and I'll forever regret that I didn't tell her to take an un-choreographed flying leap.

Yes, fame can be a bitch, as *CSI* cast member Gary Dourdan learned.

When he attacked a video paparazzo in Hollywood in 2007, I had to chuckle how times had changed.

Above: 1966 LVHS Varsity Cheer. Toni Basil, 2nd from right.
Photo: 1966 LV HS yearbook "Echo"

Dourdan, who plays a Las Vegas crime scene investigator in the long-running CBS hit series, attracted a number of photographers when he pulled up to the West Hollywood hotspot Hyde on his motorcycle.

He got upset when a video camera was pointed at him and he ordered the photographer to turn off the camera. The photographer pointed the camera to the ground. Video footage showed Dourdan going after the photographer, violently slamming him to the pavement. He clearly didn't want the exposure.

Below: From self-promotion to paparazzi beatdown, *CSI* actor Gary Dourdan.
Photo: Monty Brinton/CBS

I don't know Dourdan, but not long after I arrived in Las Vegas to write the "Vegas Confidential" column, *CSI* came in to do some shooting. A message popped up on my laptop with a sighting: Dourdan "with a beautiful blonde at a table at the Grand Lux restaurant at The Venetian."

Hoping to get more information, I emailed back, asking if the tipster worked at the Grand Lux.

"No," came the response, "this is Gary."

It was the first of many self-sightings called in by a celebrity or by his or her representative.

CHAPTER 8 – Classic Sightings

I f I had a time machine, vintage Vegas would be one of my obsessions. Type "1960s" and "Sinatra" into a search engine and see what comes up.

I'd retrace the steps of the Rat Pack. And wouldn't you love a list of sightings of then-Senator John F. Kennedy when he was in Las Vegas? We know he was hanging out with the Rat Pack in February 1960, raising money for his month-old presidential campaign. And we know he was at Sinatra's table at the Sands lounge when he became infatuated with a black-haired beauty named Judith Exner and that a month later she was the mistress he shared with the mob.

Bottom line: An overzealous gossip columnist wouldn't have lasted long in those days. Not with the mob and Sinatra calling the shots in Vegas. But that was then, this is now, and these are my favorites from the past few years of sightings in my newspaper column.

Los Angeles Lakers star Kobe Bryant, snacking on frozen grapes in July 2007 at Bare pool lounge, the topless venue at The Mirage. When he returned to Las Vegas for the Olympics qualifying rounds, his wife, Vanessa, joined him. . . .

Amid the swirl of a festivity-packed week marking Planet Hollywood's official name-change in 2007 (to shed the old Aladdin name), All-Star pitcher Roger Clemens found a tranquil place to keep his arm in shape. The seven-time Cy Young Award winner rose above it all, warming up on the roof, 43 stories above the Strip. . . .

Above: Jeff Gordon
Photo: KM Cannon/*Review-Journal*

Below: Rodney Dangerfield
Photo: Jeff Scheid/*Review-Journal*

NASCAR star Jeff Gordon, spotted jumping into an old-school dance contest at 1 a.m. at Body English in the Hard Rock Hotel. He was in it to win it: He wowed the crowd with two backflips and a helicopter move. . . .

The last time I saw Rodney Dangerfield, in September 2001, he was weaving through the casino crowd at the MGM Grand at 3 a.m. on a motorized scooter, waving off pursuing autograph hounds. He was also wearing pajamas. . . .

NFL Hall of Famer Jerry Rice, lighting up the dance floor on a Sunday night at Pure inside Caesars Palace in 2007. *The Dancing With the Stars* contestant headed for the dance floor after signing autographs in the VIP section. . . .

Three-time Grammy winner Jon Secada, surprising his wife Maritere, by joining the Chippendale dancers at the Rio. It was part of their 10th anniversary weekend in 2007. . . .

Barry Manilow, pulling Regis Philbin onstage for a duet of "Can't Smile Without You," during Manilow's show at the Las Vegas Hilton in January 2006. . . .

Saturday Night Live great Dana Carvey had the cast and crew of *Love* roaring with his Paul McCartney imitation during a 2006 backstage visit at The Mirage. . . .

Broadway icon Harvey Fierstein and the cast of *Hairspray* showing up en masse to see Rock and Roll Hall of Famer Ruth Brown perform at the Bootlegger Bistro in 2006. Among the *Hairspray* crowd was Fran Jaye who played Motormouth Maybelle in the musical, the role Brown created in the original 1988 movie. . . .

Cut off at the pass: Secret Service agents

Tom Jones Mystery Solved?

Tom Jones' anatomy has had 'em buzzing for decades.

A member (and yes that's what we're talking about here) of Jones' band finally gathered enough nerve to ask Jones about it, I'm told.

The Welsh superstar explained it this way: It's not what people think. He merely rearranges the total package in such a way as to create the illusion that he's the second coming of Milton Berle.

Photo: Courtesy Planet Hollywood

Above: Barkley, workin' it.
Photo: Courtesy Light

Below: Lucky Jessica.
Photo: ⓒMaggiejumps

sensed a clear and present danger during Bill Clinton's Halloween dinner at the Palms' N9NE Steakhouse. Making a beeline toward Clinton was hard-partying rocker Vince Neil, dressed as NASCAR racer Rusty Wallace, and his wife Lia, whose skimpy mermaid outfit set off all sorts of alarms for the agents. With careers on the line, the costumed couple was turned away. . . .

Charles Barkley, while partying with Tiger Woods at the Bellagio's Light club, got the house rocking when he climbed on the stage and worked the stripper pole with some ladies during the NBA All-Star Weekend in 2007. . . .

Jessica Biel, playing a hunch at an MGM Grand blackjack table on a date with Derek Jeter. One of my spies said Biel decided to hit with a 12, with the dealer showing a 6. Jeter gave her a look and she said, "You always told me to play my hunches." She got a 4, and again stuck with her hunch. A 3 gave her a 19 and she stood. The dealer went bust. A player at the table leaned over and told Jeter, "I'd rather be lucky than smart." Jeter, who had split 9s and also won, replied, "Always.". . . .

At the height of the 2005 Congressional hearings on steroid abuse in Major League Baseball, New York Yankees slugger Jason Giambi let his feelings be known. He wore a t-shirt with the words, "Better Living Through Chemistry" to Body English, the Hard Rock Hotel nightclub. A photo of Giambi in the t-shirt was posted on a popular nightlife website, but was mysteriously pulled within hours. . . .

Actor Kiefer Sutherland, posing for photos in 2007 with former dominatrix and Nevada gubernatorial candidate Leola McConnell, better known as Mistress Lee, outside a third floor room about 3 a.m. during a swingers convention at the Hard Rock Hotel. . . .

Tom Cruise and Katie Holmes were spotted kissing at Cirque du Soleil's *KÀ* show at the MGM Grand mere days after going public with their romance in 2006. Not everyone was buying it. "What kind of sham is this?" CNN's Bill Hemmer said on *American Morning*. He added, "You are gullible, America.". . . .

Lindsay Lohan and bad-girl rapper Eve unveiled the latest in ankle accessories — the alcohol-monitoring kind — during Las Vegas visits in 2007. Lohan sported hers in July, a day after she completed a six-week stint of residential and extended care treatment at a Malibu rehab center. Eve wore hers in September during the *MTV Video Music Awards*. Lohan made her appearance at Pure nightclub, where she had planned to hold her 21st birthday party on July 2. Eve had her anklet removed at The Mirage's Fix restaurant after 45 days of sobriety and celebrated with a vodka soda and a splash of cranberry. . . .

British soccer star David Beckham and his wife Victoria — a.k.a. "Posh Spice" of the Spice Girls — checked out Sin City's sexy side during a December 2007 visit to a

Above: Lohan visited Vegas sporting an alcohol monitoring anklet.

Photo: Seth Wenig/AP

Father Knows Best?

The late Bill Miller is best remembered as a key player in Elvis' comeback. The former entertainment director of the Sahara and International Hotel (now the Las Vegas Hilton) is also known for being the father of former controversial *New York Times* reporter Judith Miller. His colorful background might explain why his daughter didn't want to be perceived as a snitch. She served 85 days in jail for refusing to testify before a federal grand jury investigating the exposure of CIA agent Valerie Plame. According to Radar magazine's website, Bill Miller had a number of close Cosa Nostra associates. "Everyone knew Bill Miller was all mobbed-up," recalled retired NYPD Lieutenant Joseph Coffey, the former head of the New York State Organized Crime Task Force.

Sahara carpet photo: David G. Schwartz

Above: Victoria Beckham aka Posh Spice performs with the Spice Girls at Mandalay Bay, December 2007.

Photo: ☺ Kate-aen

private room at Spearmint Rhino, the popular adult entertainment club. When the Beckhams walked through the club, I'm told the dancers were in such hot pursuit it looked like a jail break. . . .

The Beckhams were in town for a long weekend that included the Floyd Mayweather-Ricky Hatton title fight and three concerts by the reunited Spice Girls. The Beckhams' strip club outing came a night after dinner with Tom Cruise and Katie Holmes at SW Steakhouse at Wynn Las Vegas. . . .

Zaniness ruled at the premiere of *Monty Python's Spamalot* at Wynn Las Vegas in March 2007. The highlight of the after-party came when the show's creator, Eric Idle, and John O'Hurley, who played King Arthur, launched into a lively ballroom dance as a deejay played the Beatles' "When I'm Sixty-Four.". . . .

Earlier, on the red — make that, cowhide-print — carpet at the show's premiere, Diane Sawyer (who is married to Mike Nichols, the show's director) commandeered a microphone from an in-house camera crew and conducted an interview with Python animator-turned-director Terry Gilliam. . . .

Former *Saturday Night Live* cast member Kevin Nealon caught the bouquet from female lead Nikki Crawford at the end of the premiere. Well-trained, he quickly handed the flowers over to his wife, actress Susan Yeagley. . . .

A week or so earlier, Idle had proved he would do whatever it takes to keep *Spamalot* fans entertained. When a technical glitch stopped the show, he jumped onstage and entertained the crowd with about ten minutes of stand-up comedy and banter with Nichols. . . .

Former Coors Brewing Co. Chairman Bill Coors, still spry and witty at 90, having a bottle of Coors delivered to his table at Restaurant Guy Savoy by one of the distributors who was in town for the beer company's 2007 distributor convention. Coors was in town with his wife Rita and delivered the keynote speech to the general session at Caesars Palace. . . .

Elton John, joining Prince on-stage for a rendition of the Beatles' classic, "The Long and Winding Road," at Prince's 3121 club inside the Rio during the NBA All-Star Game Weekend in 2007. . . .

Dealers at the Palms are accustomed to seeing celebrities flock through the property. No big deal. . . .

But the sight of the towering basketball star Yao Ming strolling through the casino during All-Star media day was too much. "We had dealers drop their cards and leave their tables to go over and see Yao when he walked through," said Gavin Maloof, who is co-owner of the Sacramento Kings and part of the family that owns the Palms. "We probably lost two or three thousand dollars.". . . .

Above: Sir Elton John performed with Prince during the 2007 NBA All-Star Game Weekend.
Photo: KM Cannon/ *Review-Journal*

Dirk Nowitzki of the Dallas Mavericks, Steve Nash of the Phoenix Suns, and Mavs owner Mark Cuban all made it to the Hofbrauhaus beer garden for the wedding reception of Nowitzki's sister, Silke. The 7-foot German center borrowed a guitar during the party and joined Hofbrauhaus musicians in serenading the bride and groom. They toasted the couple by clinking supersized steins and singing, "In Munich Stands a Hofbrauhaus — one, two, three!". . . .

Above: Siegfried and Roy.
Photo: Cara Roberts

Above: Footwear-less and fancy-free model Petra Nemkova.
Photo: Courtesy Pure Group

Siegfried and Roy gave seven-time Tour de France winner Lance Armstrong and his three children a two-and-a-half-hour behind-the-scenes tour of their Secret Garden animal habitat at The Mirage in June 2007. . . .

Al Pacino and his brother-in-law Mark, in the crowd at the Air Supply concert at The Orleans in 2007. They arrived during the second song and left before the lights came up, but Mark sent a note backstage that read "Al loved the show!". . . .

Harrison Ford and Calista Flockhart at *O* on November of 2006. Later, backstage, Ford put on a clown nose and hat and posed with cast members. . . .

Herschel Walker, the 1982 Heisman Trophy winner, working out at the Ultimate Fighting Championship gym a couple of miles west of the Strip before attending a UFC event at the Hard Rock Hotel in November 2006. He told *Review-Journal* sports writer Kevin Iole that he's a big fan of boxing and mixed martial arts and has a black belt in tae kwon do and jujitsu. . . .

Petra Nemkova, the Czech supermodel who survived the 2004 tsunami in the Indian Ocean, dancing barefoot at Wynn Las Vegas' Tryst club in October 2006. . . .

The Reverend Al Sharpton sipping a brand of bottled Liquid Salvation water at OPM nightclub next to Caesars Palace during a 2006 visit. . . .

Pamela Anderson, triggering a paparazzi stampede when she stepped into one of Tao nightclub's marble tubs full of rose petals with Jesus Villa, the horned satyr from Cirque du Soleil's sexy *Zumanity* show. . . .

Verne Troyer, better known as Mini-Me in the Austin Powers movies, shopping at Gap Kids in a shopping mall along the Strip. . . .

Former supermodel and reality TV star Janice Dickinson getting lap dances for herself and pals at Seamless strip club. . . .

Jennifer Lopez and Mark Anthony, celebrating his 38th birthday, in the front row of Juan Gabriel's concert at the Colosseum at Caesars Palace in 2006. . . .

Did she need the weekend to catch up? Actress-rapper Shar Jackson, who had two children with Kevin Federline, attended the *Chippendales* male dance revue five times in one week in 2007. . . .

Michael Jordan arriving in time for the 2006 Pole-a-Palooza stripper contest at Light inside the Bellagio. . . .

Seattle Seahawks head coach Mike Holmgren still had the big game on his mind while attending *Mamma Mia!* the week after Seattle lost the 2006 Super Bowl to Pittsburgh. From his fifth row seats where he would have heard every word of "The Winner Takes It All," he was overheard telling a guest, "I'm just trying to get over Sunday.". . . .

Members of the band Pantera, toasting their late guitarist "Dimebag" Darrell Abbott, with shots of Crown Royal at the Rainbow Bar & Grill on what would have been his 39th birthday in August 2005. Abbott was killed the previous December when an audience member jumped onstage and shot him during a show in Columbus, Ohio. Joining Pantera in the toast was Slash from Velvet Revolver. . . .

Above: Charles Barkley is no match for Mini-Me, Verne Troyer.
Photo: Jeff Scheid/ *Review-Journal*

Above: Bright Lights, Big City - Kidman seen here with husband Keith Urban likes the glow of Vegas.
Photo: Jeremy Lyverse/Review-Journal

Too many vampire movies? In September 2004, after Nicole Kidman attended the Oscar De La Hoya-Bernard Hopkins fight at the MGM Grand Garden, she stopped at the Palms to check out the rooftop ghostbar, then headed back to Los Angeles by limo. I'm told the ride cost $800. She spent two hours at ghostbar and fell in love with the view. Palms owner George Maloof offered a suite, but she declined, saying, "I love the nights in Las Vegas but I don't like the mornings.". . . .

Comedian Andy Dick, a runaway comet himself, tried Flyaway Indoor Skydiving in 2007. . . .

Gennaro Gattuso, a starter on the World Cup winning Italian team of 2006 — which put together a closing un-beaten streak of 25 games — partied at Fix and Caramel

in the Bellagio not long after the decisive game. . . .

Manchester United soccer star Wayne Rooney partied at the Hard Rock Hotel's Rehab pool party while in town for countryman Ricky Hatton's fight against Jose Luis Castillo in June 2007. Rooney also dined at Tao Asian Bistro inside the Venetian, near Boston Red Sox slugger David Ortiz and NBA veteran Jalen Rose. . . .

Actor Michael Madsen of *Tilt*, *Reservoir Dogs*, and *Sin City*, popped up in the Pioneer Saloon in rural Goodsprings to change from casual to a suit coat and black and red boots. He posed for a photo with the bartender

Above: Michael Madsen – quick change artist
Photo: David Giesbrecht/ESPN

Above: Gene Simmons and his tongue.
Photo: John Locher/ *Review-Journal*
Below: Tribute band, "Tiny Kiss."
Photo: Jane Kalinowsky/ *Review-Journal*

and then split. Madsen had filmed *The Winner* there in 1996. . . .

Jason Alexander, best known as George Costanza on *Seinfeld*, got a big laugh before the Amazing Johnathan show even started. During the pre-show audience scan with a video camera, Alexander was shown in his seat with the following caption on the video screen: "Thinks he's George from *Seinfeld*.". . . .

Gene Simmons of Kiss, being swarmed by members of Tiny Kiss, a little people tribute group, during his reality show shoot at the Hard Rock Hotel's pool cabanas. . . .

Michael Jackson: A falling star finds a crash pad

Las Vegas has become Michael Jackson's second home, whether anyone really likes it or not.

His parents, Joe and Katherine, have owned a home here for years and several of his siblings have lived in Las Vegas off and on. Some of his family members once attempted to build a casino and production facility on land where the Palms now stands.

During the 1990s, Michael was a regular at The Mirage, where it was rumored that Steve Wynn was courting Jackson for a headliner run. He wrote an original theme song for Mirage headliners Siegfried and Roy, whom he had been friends with since he was a teenager. (The Jackson Five performed in the original MGM Grand's headliner showroom while the illusionists were next door in *Hallelujah Hollywood*.)

Above: From one Neverland to another–Jocko tries to relaunch his career in Vegas.
Photo: Todd Bennett/AP

But the welcome cooled when Jackson's problems started surfacing.

He started popping up on a regular basis in 2002, while British journalist Martin Bashir was filming the controversial documentary, *Living With Michael Jackson*, which aired in 2003. Cameras followed along for jaw-dropping shopping sprees around Las Vegas. Later, we learned it was all show. The money-crunched superstar was having the goods returned days later.

He spent a lot of time here in 2003, and his return to Las Vegas from Santa Barbara on the day he was booked on suspicion of child molestation created a media circus. The slow-speed car chase was covered from the air and ground, bringing back memories of OJ Simpson's white Bronco run.

Jackson temporarily went into hiding at the Green Valley Ranch and the Ritz-Carlton at Lake Las Vegas before moving back to Neverland to await trial. After being exonerated in June 2005, he left the country for 18 months, splitting time between Dubai and Ireland before flying to Las Vegas on Christmas Eve 2006 with his children.

His apparent plan was to make a comeback in Las Vegas, but it never got off the ground. "Too radioactive," was the term I kept hearing.

He ended a six-month stay in June, leaving a multimillion-dollar, ten-bedroom rental home in Summerlin in "filthy" shambles, according to an eyewitness.

Piles of junk were left on the curb outside the home, and two Christmas trees draped with ornaments were still in place inside the house. "They left the Christmas trees up like it was still December," said my source.

Jackson had worn out his welcome at The Mirage, having left his suite in even worse condition after a lengthy stay several years earlier, sources said.

Bathrooms and bedrooms at the home on Monte Cristo Way were left in squalid condition, with children's handprints on many walls, stains on carpets, and garbage left in sinks. Jackson's three children slept together on mattresses placed on the floor of one bedroom dominated by a giant carpet stain.

During his stay in Las Vegas, Jackson was often seen taking his children to local attractions. He showed up one day with all three of his children, all unveiled, for a VIP tour of *Bodies . . . The Exhibition* at the Tropicana.

Jackson stopped at one point to lecture his children on the evils of smoking after they viewed a smoker's lung. Later, he stressed the importance of healthy eating.

After taking a tour of *Titanic: The Artifact Exhibition*, they stopped in the gift shop and purchased everything from a 33-inch skeleton to anatomy and pathology books to T-shirts featuring bones, brains, and a replica statue of The Thinker.

He returned to Las Vegas in late 2007 and was spotted at a suburban Barnes & Noble bookstore with numerous square bandages between his mouth and chin.

Hoping to cash in on the celebrity club-hosting craze over the holidays, Jackson had his people make overtures to several nightspots about bringing him in for six figures. But he got no takers.

A major development did start taking shape in early 2008. Colony Capital CEO Tom Barrack, an investment banker who had become a major investor in the

Las Vegas Hilton a few years earlier, began secret discussions with Jackson.

In May came a surprising announcement: Barrack agreed to purchase the loan on Jackson's Neverland Ranch, a $23 million bailout that was viewed as Jackson's first step toward the career comeback.

Barrack was quoted in the *Wall Street Journal* as saying, "We've been having discussions with Mr. Jackson about a recapitalization and refinancing of Neverland in addition to various other business opportunities and mutual interests."

Amid rumors that something was afoot with the Jackson family was immediate speculation that those "mutual interests" involved an Elvis-esque revival at the same hotel where Elvis jumpsuit-started his career almost 40 years ago.

Postscript: Know your celebrities

News of Sophia Loren's arrival had 'em buzzing at Maggiano's Little Italy. The room was electric as she made a grand entrance with an entourage and Fashion Show Mall security. "The whole nine yards," Maggiano's general manager John Gerarde said.

But it wasn't Sophia, the toast of Italy. It was an im-pasta. Welcome to Las Vegas, the faux capital of the universe, where phonies are constantly out to land a freebie by snookering local businesses. "We're in a city where you have to look twice," Gerarde said.

A longtime event handler agreed with Gerarde. "We've had Snoop Doggs and Britneys show up and ask for comps." Even people portraying B-listers, said my source. "We've had people call and claim, 'I'm so-and-so's accountant, people claiming to be agents, demanding comps.'"

CHAPTER 9 – Behind the Celebrity and Nightclub Scene

How it all works

Las Vegas has been using celebrities as bait since mobster Bugsy Siegel flew in movie stars for the December 26, 1946 opening of the Flamingo, the casino that pointed the way to the future of the Strip.

Hordes of locals turned out, many of them dressed to the nines and others in the cowboy boots and hats that characterized life away from the Strip.

The star power of the hour included comedian Jimmy Durante and his sidekick Eddie Jackson, magician Tommy Wonder, and Xavier Cugat's Latin big band with singer Rose Marie. I interviewed Rose Marie after her induction into the Casino Legends Hall of Fame in October 2001. Las Vegas, she said, gave little indication it would soon become the entertainment capital of the world.

"The first two nights, the place was filled with people who came to see celebrities like Clark Gable and many others. On the third night, the celebrities left and there were nine people in the audience."

Celebrities have always loved Las Vegas and tourists have always loved seeing celebrities in Las Vegas. A match made in heaven.

Down-and-out boxing champ Joe Louis was on the payroll at Caesars Palace for years as an on-site attraction — officially a "greeter" — even when his health failed and he needed a wheelchair.

Celebrities might pour in for a big fight, but no one was paying them much, if anything — certainly not

monster money — to show up at a resort opening or to
host a private party for high rollers. During that long
run in the '70s and '80s when Vegas was more kitsch
than cool, it was better for younger stars to keep any
association low-key.

That attitude continued all the way to the opening of
The Mirage on November 22, 1989, a date often mentioned as the city's turning point. There was no red
carpet or celebrity scene, recalls Alan Feldman, longtime
vice president of public relations for Mirage developer
Steve Wynn.

"Any celebrities who came to The Mirage were not flown
in, not paid for," said Feldman. "They came because The
Mirage was a very cool place. Siegfried and Roy were
a very big draw. Steve was pretty strict about that. His

attitude was, 'We'll give you the time of your life, but you're going to pay.'"

Financier Michael Milken was among the handful of recognizable people, "and not as recognizable as a few years later," said Feldman, referring to Milken's notoriety and two-year prison stint for illegal securities trading in 1990. His junk bond funding provided the fuel to build the new Las Vegas, but Milken's securities fraud sank about four dozen savings and loan associations.

Siegfried and Roy and their white tigers were the anchor entertainment act at the Mirage. Wynn has said that no musical performer of the day was willing or able to make a nightly commitment to the new property. So he decided to build upon the illusionists' popularity at the nearby Frontier hotel, building a lavish new revue around them. Wynn so believed in his stars that he symbolically had the duo checked in as the hotel's first guests.

Above: Among the celebrities taking in Barbra Streisand's concert at the grand opening of the Planet Hollywood Resort in November 2007 was Patrick Swayze with Lisa Niemi. Swayze was diagnosed with pancreatic cancer two months later.
Photo: Denise Truscello/Courtesy Planet Hollywood

When the Bellagio opened nine years later, "among the things that changed was Vegas itself," said Feldman. The new MGM Grand existed, the Venetian and Mandalay Bay were close to opening. This time Wynn "had quite a list for the opening," said Feldman. "Rooms, food, and beverage would have been comped. I don't recall us sending a plane."

Still, even in 1998, "There was no red carpet per se. The

closest we got was Cirque had a camera crew and picked out celebrities and asked them about the show. They had a camera in the lobby and were just picking people off," Feldman recalls.

"It's gone Hollywood, but everybody's gone Hollywood," he says of today's red carpet-saturated scene. "Look through the pages of magazines and you'll see step-and-repeats, which have become completely normal at events." In those days, the term was rarely heard in Las Vegas, even in high-level PR circles.

Below: George Maloof transformed the celebrity scene.
Photo: Cara Roberts

"I remember ordering the first of those," Feldman said, "and I didn't know you called the banner (displaying the sponsoring logo behind the celebrity) the 'step-and-repeat.'"

Today no self-respecting new club would think of having an opening-night red carpet event without a step-and-repeat banner, chock full of sponsor plugs.

The trigger point

A seismic shift occurred in November 2001 when the opening of the Palms ushered in a new era of celebrity.

George Maloof, a 36-year-old upstart in a city of big-time operators, was taking the biggest gamble of his young life.

One of the youngest members of the Maloof family, George had left his hometown of Albuquerque, New Mexico in 1982

and headed for Trinity College in San Antonio, Texas. He dabbled in general courses and majored in football. By his junior year, he was the school's starting quarterback.

He was preparing to return to Trinity after the summer break when he had a career-altering conversation with a family friend, former FBI agent Jim Doyle, who headed security for the Maloofs. They talked about Las Vegas, where Doyle had worked with the FBI. "He knew I loved Las Vegas," said Maloof.

The more they talked, the more Maloof, 20, found himself fascinated with the idea of chasing his dream in the city of chance.

Still searching for his eureka moment, Maloof, on a whim, booked a flight to Las Vegas the next day to check out the University of Nevada, Las Vegas. Upon arriving, he checked into the Imperial Palace, in the heart of The Strip. "My room was next to the 'P' and I walked out on the balcony. I remember thinking, 'If I came to college here, maybe I could own one of these.'"

He went back to New Mexico, packed and headed back to Las Vegas. "It was a very impulsive decision. It literally happened overnight."

He enrolled in hotel management and worked at the front desk of the Fremont Hotel and in a training program at La Mirage, a motel at Flamingo and Paradise. It was about that time La Mirage had its 15 minutes of fame, when resort developer Steve Wynn purchased the name for $250,000 so he could use the Mirage name for his upcoming project.

Soon Maloof's dream to own a casino started to take shape. He began looking around town in search of a site. "It took a year and a half," he said, before he found 14 acres in North Las Vegas, well off the beaten path and a world away from the Strip. "I'd been hanging out in small casinos. I understood the locals market," he said.

Finding a piece of property was easy compared to finding a lender. "I got denied a ton over four years. I probably met 50 different lenders," he recalled. Maloof was too young, they said, and didn't have the experience.

Finally, he found a banker who would give him a $20 million loan, but there were strings attached. "My brothers, sister, and mother had to sign a personal guarantee," he said.

And he had to learn the gaming business first, the banker said.

So Maloof moved to Central City, Colorado, where he purchased the Central Palace casino in 1990. He spent two years there before moving back to Las Vegas to open the Fiesta, which was built for $10 million.

Maloof ran it from 1994 to 2000, when he sold it to the family-owned Station Casinos for more than $180 million. Not bad for his first business venture in a city dominated by the big boys. With the proceeds, he built the $265 million, 430-room Palms about a half-mile west of the Strip.

He had located that site in the mid-1990s, and had serious competition from two interested parties: "One was another gaming company," said Maloof, "and Michael Jackson was looking at a piece of it. His land would have been where half the Palms is now." (Some of Michael Jackson's money was behind an earlier proposal for the land by other family members. Developers working with his brothers touted a casino and entertainment complex called the Jackson Family's Destiny before the Jacksons fell out of the picture in 1993.)

Maloof bought the 32-acre site in 1997 for $27 million, using a straw buyer when another company didn't proceed. A straw buyer can purchase property for another person in order to conceal the identity of the real purchaser. His timing was perfect. Not ten years later, land on the Strip was cracking the $30 million-an-acre barrier, with the New Frontier and its 38 acres going for a reported $33 million per acre to New York-based El Ad Properties.

Maloof was banking on the locals to continue supporting his generous slot returns at the Palms, but he also had another element in mind.

"I knew there was a public fascination with celebrity," he said over sushi one night at KOI inside Planet Hollywood. "I was always interested in having a celebrity hotspot that would cater to celebrities. We took a page out of Hollywood," he said, referring to star power that fueled the legendary hotspots from the heyday of the Brown Derby, Chasens, and Ciro's, on into the era of Spago.

Maloof also saw what was happening at the Hard Rock Hotel, which carved out a new casino demographic previously not seen on the Strip, or at not least in such density as the suddenly high-profile young hipsters clustered around the Hard Rock's center bar. Hard Rock developer Peter Morton lured celebrities such as Nicolas Cage to town for the hotel's opening weekend in March 1995 by booking the Eagles for an exclusive concert (no tickets sold to the public). His music venue The Joint eschewed the traditional showroom layout for a rock club vibe.

Peter Morton had a friendly rivalry going with his younger brother, Michael, who that same year became a partner in a freestanding nightclub called Drink a few blocks east of the Hard Rock. George Maloof was a good customer, and when Drink ran afoul of its residential neighbors, he convinced Morton and partner Scott De-Graff to join a more welcoming casino environment by opening a nightclub (Rain), ultralounge (ghostbar) and

Party Time

The Palms and N9NE Group had a key ally in landing the world's first new Playboy Club in the world since 1984. Playboy founder Hugh Hefner said his long time association with Peter Morton's father, Arnie, was a factor in the Palms–N9NE deal, helping to make it "the perfect partnership."

Morton, who died in early 2005, was one of Hefner's original partners and a vice president for 15 years before taking off on his own with the Morton's steakhouse concept.

To get the word out about everything inside his new casino, Maloof threw a party at the Playboy Mansion in California a month before the Palms opened, inviting many of Hollywood's hot names.

restaurant (N9NE steakhouse) at the Palms. Maloof ended up designing a casino that was half Hard Rock — the clubs and restaurants on the east end — and half Fiesta, with a movie theater and food court for locals on the west end.

For opening night, November 15, 2001, Maloof went out of his way to make a celebrity statement. Among the dozens of stars on hand was a 20-year-old blonde decked out in a black dress adorned with $1 million in $100, $500 and $1,000 gaming chips.

Her name was Paris Hilton.

Almost overnight, the Palms became the hottest celebrity scene in years. A-listers poured in to check out N9NE Steak House, Little Buddha, ghostbar and Rain nightclubs. That was just the beginning. Up on the 28th floor, Maloof had quietly created a suite out of six rooms to serve as the 3,000-square-foot home for MTV's *Real World* cast and crew. The subsequent buzz around the Palms was unbelievable. I took notice when more and more friends of mine from out-of-state wanted to visit the Palms because their teenagers knew all about it from *Real World*.

Before Maloof opened the Palms, I had talked to him by telephone once or twice, but I do not recall meeting him until he invited me on a hard-hat media tour of the Palms a few months before the opening. Near the end of tour, as we were chatting, he asked if there was anything he could do to help.

That was Maloof's style. Instead of asking how he could get mentions in the column, he asked what he could do for me.

I made a modest request for some sightings. Soon they began flowing like champagne on New Year's weekend. Two years earlier, I couldn't buy a sighting.

Within a matter of months, the epicenter of the Las

Bunny Tales

Shortly after the opening of the first Playboy Club in 25 years, cotton-tail fever was running rampant. "People are offering to buy our bunny ears, cufflinks, and tails," said Heidi Wheeler, a bunny-dealer. Another Bunny-dealer Maya Kilam added, "I've had guys pull my tail off and run for the elevator."

"I've been offered $100 for my ears," Wheeler added. Sharla Jensen said ladies inquired about how they could buy the outfits. Some of the bunnies weren't prepared for the frenzy of attention.

"We were grabbed and groped all night (on opening night)," said a Bunny who asked that her name not be used. "We should put squeaky toys in our tails just to shock people," added Jensen.

Some nights were downright jaw dropping.

Bunny dealer Lindsey Roeper put on her poker face when an older man's dentures fell out of his mouth.

Vegas celebrity scene had moved off the Strip, away from the Hard Rock, and the corporate giants were not the only ones who noticed the tipping point.

The competition

A week before the Palms' opening night bash, another new nightclub, Coyote Ugly, held its VIP opening at New York-New York, in a former cigar store fronted by George Hamilton. Based on the movie of the same name, Coyote Ugly and its bar-top dancing were a smoking success. Eighteen months later, New York-New York president Felix Rappaport called it "per square foot the most successful bar in the U.S."

It wasn't big enough to be competition for local heavyweights like C2K, the short-lived but influential club at The Venetian, or Rain at the Palms, RA at Luxor, Studio 54 at the MGM Grand or Baby's at the Hard Rock, which collectively represented the first wave of nightclubs being folded under casino roofs. "Seven years ago we couldn't beg casinos to put in clubs," a top exec told me in early 2008. "Now the main attraction for people over 21 is to come to Vegas for the nightclubs."

But Coyote Ugly was nonetheless an impressive start for first-time partners Robert Frey and Steve Davidovici, who had big plans. Frey came from one of Las Vegas' best-known families; his stepfather, Irwin Molasky, was a chance-taker and a key figure in the development of Las Vegas, guiding to completion such early suburban landmarks as the Boulevard Mall and Sunrise Hospital.

Davidovici was a tough amateur boxer from Brooklyn who came to Las Vegas to tend bar in 1991. A doorman's job at Club Rio led to a five-year run as general manager in what was the first major nightclub in a Las Vegas casino, although it was technically a showroom that converted into a club in the late evening.

"I had no experience at running nightclubs," said

Frey, who was a partner at the time in Cigar Box and a partner in Sidebar Spirits, the parent company of Montecristo rum.

"I knew Stevie from Club Rio and he was the best club operator in town. I ran into him and ran it (a partnership offer) by him." They teamed up, with Davidovici providing the operational know-how and the marketing experience. He had opened RA at Luxor and helped Mandalay Bay Group open rumjungle and the Foundation Room, among others.

He also might have been the first to pioneer a concept new to Las Vegas nightlife: bottle service, which means you have to buy a bottle to sit in a VIP section. He saw it done in New York and borrowed the idea. Now it's the engine that drives many clubs into stratospheric revenue territory, with some clubs reporting that it accounts for about 50 percent of the take.

After Coyote Ugly took off, Frey, Davidovici and their partners added Hush, an open-air club atop the Polo Towers. In 2002 they added Bikinis Beach & Dance Club at the Rio. But they had their eyes on a much bigger project, a huge space at Caesars Palace called Caesars Magical Empire. Casino management had been soliciting proposals for a new tenant to take over the underperforming dinner show, modeled on Hollywood's Magic Castle, and at one point a Latin-themed club linked to Gloria Estefan and Jimmy Smits seemed to have the lock.

"It took us about a year to raise money for Pure," said Davidovici, "because no one believed in the space." In the meantime, they continued expanding, opening Tangerine at Treasure Island in July 2004. On December 31, 2004 they finally opened Pure, a 40,000-square foot monstrosity that included a stunning terrace overlooking Las Vegas Boulevard. The celebrity investors included

Above: Mariah Carey hosted Pure's grand opening, marking a new direction for grand openings at Vegas clubs.
Photo: ☺David Shankbone

Celine Dion, Shaquille O'Neal, Andre Agassi, and Steffi Graf.

Those of us who took the pre-opening tour left wondering if such a cavernous venue could work.

Pure's opening was notable for another reason. It marked the full-scale escalation of the nightclub wars. Pure had paid pop diva Mariah Carey to host the evening and perform the countdown.

"You want to open up with a bang," explained Frey, "and she was coming out with another album." The strategy worked so well, "We had 5,000 people show up," said Davidovici. "I think this was the first time a celebrity opened a club in Las Vegas."

Perhaps so, but shipping in celebrities to lure high rollers has long been a Las Vegas tradition. And on that same night, Anna Nicole Smith was at the nearby Aladdin for a VIP event put together by new owner Robert Earl, the founder of the Planet Hollywood restaurant chain.

Soon Paris Hilton, Britney Spears, Lindsey Lohan, and Pamela Anderson were up for bid, netting six figure offers for three hours of work. "Everybody said we were crazy, but we've been on every network in the country for over a year. That's how crazy we are," said Davidovici. That year began with Britney being assisted out of Pure shortly after delivering the New Year's Eve 2006 countdown.

No one can question the results. The celebrity-host strategy has become the gift that keeps on giving.

"Any time a major story comes out about Paris or Britney, they're on TV and there's a Pure logo behind them (in the stock footage)," said Davidovici. "Paris was paid to do New Year's Eve at LAX," said Davidovici, referring to Pure Management Group's next mega-club, which opened at Luxor in late 2007. "But she was in the club 19 times."

The success of giant clubs such as Pure and Tao at The Venetian — which grossed an astounding $50 million in 2006, according to company reports — didn't just happen because of the magnetic pull of celebrity hosts, he said.

"We saw Light (at the Bellagio) going with the super high-end clientele and Rain appealed to the MTV crowd," said Davidovici. Pure came up with a formula, said Davidovici, to attract and service both groups, "and I think we've been able to do that better than anybody."

They also cover every marketing base, from providing photos and video within hours of a big event, to feeding almost-instant sightings to the celebrity news outlets. It has all paid off, he said, because "people know us as the biggest nightclub group in the world," an empire that included eight clubs, three restaurants, and new projects heading into 2008.

And all of it happened in about six years. That kind of raging success rarely goes unnoticed by major corporations. "I think their goal has been to build a great brand and wait for a buyer," said a longtime Las Vegas club executive.

Another club pro saw storm clouds gathering. "We're teetering on a recession," he said, in January 2008. "I think there's a bubble," he said. "There has to be. Only so many people can afford a $500 bottle. And those people who can afford them aren't here every week."

The very next month, another party pooper known as

the Internal Revenue Service raided the offices of the Pure Management Group, Pure Nightclub, and sister club LAX at Luxor. The feds had taken no formal action as this book went to press. But the raid brought to light tales of customer hustles, and speculation that much of the cash wasn't being reported either to the government or the casino landlords.

The courtship

The courtship of celebrities starts early. The first step often begins on a Las Vegas red carpet, where many young celebrities "get their first taste of Vegas," says veteran local publicist Laura Herlovich. "They can be underage and walk the red carpet or go to a show opening, or a restaurant."

When Paris Las Vegas opened in September 1999, *Review-Journal* photographer Jeff Scheid was covering the event and a publicist asked if he wanted to take a photo of one of the VIPs. "She's going to be the next big model," Scheid recalled the publicist saying.

The publicist led the photographer to a group of older VIPS that included what appeared to be a young lady barely in her teens.

"She looked 13 and immediately started striking a pose and I thought 'Oh, please,'" said Scheid.

His photos of Paris Hilton in a Las Vegas casino might have been the first. She was 18. She was such an unknown, the photos didn't make it into the paper.

Hilton wasn't under the radar for long. George Maloof met her through her parents in 2000, about a year before he opened the Palms.

"She wasn't famous at that time. About three months before we opened, our publicist started getting calls from her, saying she wanted to attend the opening," Maloof recalls. "Then I saw her in a few magazines. She had a little following. She was just on the cusp."

Maloof thought she was "the perfect date" for the young Hollywood crowd he was wooing. "That was the whole idea," he said of asking her to walk the red carpet with him on opening night.

The age issue

Anyone under 21 in a casino or club can be a problem. Stars who aren't 21 can be a serious problem.

Maloof didn't need an opening night disaster because his "date" was under 21, so he had his publicist ask for proof of age. "We made sure she sent us verification. But she sent false verification," he said; the celebutante was still nearly nine months shy of her 21st birthday.

He got distracted and lost track of Hilton that night, but his security team kept a close eye on her.

"It's always a sensitive issue," said Maloof. "Nicky Hilton snuck into one of our clubs and we had to tell her to leave. They're used to (getting in) in Hollywood, but Vegas is different because so much is at stake."

I was walking through the Palms one night and saw Nicky Hilton walking briskly toward the casino. Behind her were three or four security types. "Stay on her," one barked.

When 18-year-old Lindsey Lohan showed up at the Palms pool in August 2004, "We reported it to gaming control and they did an investigation and took our surveillance (tapes)," Maloof says.

Below: The sneak. Nicky Hilton caught sneaking in to clubs while underage.
Photo: Cara Roberts

Above: A match made in heaven, Hugh Hefner's Playboy empire and George Maloof's Palms Casino Resort.
Photo: Cara Roberts

One night when Playboy founder Hugh Hefner was by with the three live-in girlfriends made famous in the reality series *The Girls Next Door*, they sat down at a gaming table and Kendra Wilkinson started playing.

"I found out about it later that evening, and it was a situation where Hef came in and we're assuming he knows someone is under 21 and (would not have allowed her to) play. Gaming control came in."

Maloof found himself in a reverse situation one day when I called for comment after running a sighting of him at a club at Green Valley Ranch with Lauren Conrad and Heidi Montag of MTV's hit reality show *The Hills*. A colleague in the *Review-Journal* newsroom had checked their ages and both were under twenty-one.

"When I found out, I called someone at Station Casinos. They did an internal investigation and I helped them, because they had to report it to gaming control," Maloof says. Like the Hefner situation turned back at him, "They assumed when I sat down to teach them how to play blackjack, I wouldn't bring in someone under twenty-one."

He added, "The minute you find out you violated any

kind of gaming regulation, you have to self-report or it's bad news. If you know it and allow it, you're in big trouble. And there's a lot more scrutiny now with so many cell phone cameras out there."

In July 2001, I ran an item about Britney Spears, then 19, and Justin Timberlake, 20, spending three hours in a private area at The Venetian's C2K, then the biggest club in town. C2K general manager Tye Smith told me no rules were bent because the non-gaming area was "the same thing as (underage performers) being on stage."

Even though Smith insisted no alcohol was served during the pop stars' 2:30 to 5:30 a.m. visit, his explanation didn't satisfy some hotel execs I contacted. "It's cut and dried with a nightclub," one executive said. "You have to be 21 because it's hard to control." With a show, "If you want to take your daughter to see Tom Jones, she can have a soft drink and you can have Jack Daniels."

Another said: "We've made exceptions for headliners' children at shows, but you can't have kids in a nightclub where alcohol is served." For years, someone under 21 was allowed in a club if it was a private function. That changed in early 2007, said Maloof.

If the liquor licensing officials were motivated to crack down, as some believe, it was because of Stavros Niarchos, Paris Hilton's boyfriend. He was getting into a number of clubs when he was underage. The final straw might have been when Paris scheduled a party at Tao for what was advertised as his 21st birthday.

But that changed when I reported it was his 20th birthday, not 21st.

Who gets in?

Word to the wise to all you guys out there: Your chances of getting into a Las Vegas nightclub go up exponentially based on the number of ladies you're with. Two dudes may wait in line all night. Groups of ladies fresh from a campus are usually a slam dunk.

After that come all sorts of angles. Just ask the person next to you.

Many clubs hand out thousands of passes that promise to get you in the VIP line or offer half-price admission after midnight. "There's all kinds of tricks you lure patrons with," said a well-known club operator.

Be forewarned that discounted tickets being sold by street marketers, airport pitchmen, or cabbies, with the promise of getting you into one of the hot clubs, are often a scam. You can get 'em free at any number of places.

Getting in line is the easy part. Consider yourself lucky if you get inside the club just for the cover charge. It's no secret that most clubs understand the longer the line, the higher the anxiety. That's where the line slide comes in.

"If people have been waiting all night, they're not going to go somewhere else and start over," said the operator. Club employees, usually the size of big league umpires, will go down the line and fish for people who really want to get in. The line guy might get $200, but now everyone in the group is still going to have to pay a $30 to $40 cover charge. Sometimes the doorman demands more, maybe $50 to $100 per person. Some doormen were collecting $10,000 per night.

"Pure has door guys who make more than the president," said one source, before the Internal Revenue Service raided the management group's offices in February 2008. For the record, U.S. presidents are paid $400,000 a year, plus benefits. One head doorman in town, swears my source, hauls in half a million a year, almost all of it in cash. His assistant at the door makes $300,000 and other door men top $100,000. No wonder the IRS started paying attention; the cash exchanged at the entrance of some clubs would shock the Treasury people who print it.

Club executives are well worth $500,000 a year. One can only imagine the checks going back to Pure's celebrity investors, the source said.

At another new club, one of several that opened on New Year's Eve 2007, word has it a beautiful female employee gets $700 a night to "grab attractive girls and pay them $150 to come into the club. Plus they get a bottle free. The recruiter gets $100 for every lady she brings in," a spy told me.

Getting an edge

Reporters have a better chance of hitting a Megabucks jackpot than getting Las Vegas executives to reveal the tricks of their trade. That's because, said one club operator, "The competition is more intense than I've ever seen. I mean, how many nightclubs have opened in the last ten months? Ten?"

But there are still ways to find out.

Maloof volunteered that in his early years at the Fiesta, he purchased a wig, hat, and beard and headed across the street to Texas Station to check out the competition. "I'd go over to check out their promotions, their entertainment. Some people get uptight if you walk in, so I put on the wig and the hat."

The beard was a bit much, so he passed on that. He put it away and forgot about it. Until one night when a girlfriend found the beard in a drawer in his bedroom and "gave me a funny look."

Snoopy reporters get looks, too, when you ask about the tactics being used to stay on or near the top.

High on the list of mistakes you can't make in the heated nightclub wars: Keep track of the high rollers,

VIPs, and celebrities. "If you're going to pay for someone to show up, you don't want them ending up in the sightings at someone else's place," explained one nightclub source. "People find out who's coming to town and try to poach 'em." One particular VIP host with a PhD in poaching is persona non grata at a number of properties.

Wily club operators are finding new ways to protect their investment in the superheated environment. "We had a female celebrity come into Stack one night," said a restaurant executive. "She was hosting a party at a competing nightclub the next night. The nightclub sent along one of their security guards to ensure we wouldn't set up a photo" that might end up among gossip column sightings or on TV.

Said another, "I've heard the Palms has a new policy. If I'm opening a new club, I'm not allowed to come into one of their restaurants until my place is open. They want to prevent poaching waitresses and waiters."

Below: Jeff Beacher, full of surprises.
Photo: Jane Kalinowsky/ *Review-Journal*

Hard Rock Hotel founder Peter Morton won more than his share of entertainment bidding wars with the giant properties, because, rumor had it, "he had moles."

Well-rewarded moles.

The Hard Rock also relied on Nobu restaurant — which rode strong into Las Vegas on its New York reputation as a happening celebrity haunt with a killer menu — as a recruitment tool in the poaching wars. One particular mission worked this way: a major entertainer performing at another property was targeted. Show producer Jeff Beacher, a gregarious New Yorker and friend of Morton's son Harry, worked his way up to the star after the show and mentioned dinner at Nobu. Within minutes, the big name was in a Hard Rock SUV and on his way. That's known as relationship building, Las Vegas-style.

Poaching became less of an issue when celebrities started signing clauses in their contracts that prohibited them from club-hopping. Some VIP hosts suspect that the habitual celebrity club hoppers were getting paid at every stop.

The bigger clubs have become so organized that one VIP host will mainly deal with star athletes, another with the music industry and another with Hollywood. Like reporters who concentrate on politics or a cop beat, some VIP hosts narrow their focus to cultivate their clientele list.

Paid to play

Like no other time in history, it pays to be a celebrity in Las Vegas.

Even reality show D-listers and *American Idol* also-rans were cashing in years after their 15 minutes on the nightclub gravy train, one which took off after Pure Nightclub hired Mariah Carey to host its opening night in 2004.

It quickly got out of control. Britney Spears banked between $250,000 and $300,000 for a 2006 New Year's Eve countdown gig. Hearing that, Lindsey Lohan's management requested $1 million for two appearances, which were to involve her 21st birthday party and a New Year's Eve countdown. Alas, she went into rehab shortly before her Las Vegas birthday party in July 2006, which was delayed. Paris Hilton was here every other week, it seemed, to scoop up the deals worth $150,000 or more.

Even with the substantial payouts, paid celebrity appearances seem to be working. When Carey returned three years later for the New Year's Eve that rang in 2008, word has it she got $250,000. But that was more than covered by the reported 2,500 paid admissions, many for $250 a head. Factor in the gusher of champagne sales from $500 to $1,000 a pop and you have the makings of a record-revenue night.

Sales on a good weekend night at many of the mid-size clubs like Jet and The Bank can top $100,000. The Pure group maximizes its celebrity deals by having their stars dine at their various restaurants to further push the corporate brands.

Bottle service

Know going in that bottle service is the price you pay — and then pay some more — for prime real estate in the best clubs.

A veteran club-goer explains that novices will most likely want to sit at a table. "But the club will require you to buy a bottle of alcohol for eight-to-ten times its retail value — and the club's wholesale price is approximately one half of retail — for the privilege of sitting at that table."

In addition, a charge of nearly 28% (7.75% tax and 20% gratuity) is added on top of the alcohol. So a $20 bottle of Skyy Vodka can go for $400. The tax ($31) and gratuity ($80) push the cost to $511, not including the tip to the door and VIP hosts.

The usual requirement is one bottle per three patrons. So if you have four patrons, that is a minimum of two bottles, three on weekends, possibly up to six bottles on major weekends for a table of eight people.

"Now the clubs have figured out an even bigger rip-off," our veteran explains. "The new enticement is to lure in locals (Las Vegas area residents, the bread and butter clients) with the allure of a 'free bottle,' which amounts to 'buy one, get one free.' However, it is far from free.

"Here's an incident that happened to us on a Saturday

night at one of the major clubs — take your pick because it happens at all of them.

"I was offered a free bottle. I ordered Malibu Rum and a 'free vodka,' which is normally a small bottle of Skyy. The waitress bought us a bottle of Bacardi Coconut, since they didn't have Malibu, and the Skyy. The bill was over $700. They preauthorized my credit card for $891."

Our party warrior decided to "take a hard look" and examine the bill. Here's how it broke down:

Our sticker-shocked fun seeker started to grill the server about certain items listed on the bill, about which she was clueless. "I asked, 'Why is there both a service charge and a gratuity charge? Why is the gratuity charge 40% instead of 20%?

Alcohol	$475.00
Tax	$36.81
Service Charge	$36.81
Gratuity (40%)	$190.00
Total	$738.62

"After a few minutes, she returned to inform me that the 40% is 20% for each bottle. I said that both bottles aren't $475! And that doesn't explain the service charge. Also, 'Why am I paying a service charge for a free bottle?'"

Next, a bar manager came back to explain: Every table has a four percent service charge regardless of how many bottles they order.

"I said, 'So, four percent of $475 is $19, not $36.81. You are double charging tax on a free bottle!' He told me that that's how it was explained to him.

"So I said, 'I'll make your life easy. I don't need a 'free' bottle since we're not big drinkers and I didn't order the Bacardi. So do everyone a favor. Take back the bottle of Bacardi Coconut, charge me for the Skyy vodka plus the 28% tax and gratuity and we're done.'"

They weren't. The bill returned as follows:

Alcohol (For the cheaper bottle of Skyy vodka)	$375.00
Tax	$26.16
Service Charge	$15.00
Gratuity (40%)	$150.00
Total	$566.16

So once again, our intrepid clubber asks, "Why am I being charged 40% on a single bottle?" The bill was again sent back, this time with the instructions, "Get it right!"

The final bill appeared:

Tired of the fight, the bill was signed. So, our battle-scarred clubber asks, "The question becomes, 'What's the difference between a single bottle and a buy one-get one free bottle of alcohol?'

Alcohol (For the cheaper bottle of Skyy vodka)	$375.00
Tax	$26.16
Service Charge	$15.00
Gratuity (20%)	$75.00
Total	$491.16

"According to my calculations, it's approximately $245.58."

Surveillance

Cameras aren't just checking for cheats at the gaming tables or monitoring the clubs for illegal activities. They're protecting other interests as well.

"We had an A-lister come in with his manager and they met a girl," said a major executive. A few days later, "She came back and threatened to go to the police, saying the A-lister had sexually assaulted her."

The A-lister had a big $25 million show a few weeks away; he was in a panic. "We went to the surveillance tapes and shot down her claim," he said. The tape showed the girl had gone to the manager's room. There was no sign of the star.

Surveillance tapes also helped police tie O.J. Simpson to his associates after his arrest in September 2007 on kidnapping and robbery charges at Palace Station.

Spy cameras also are showing up above the VIP sections of many of the clubs. "That's probably to protect the club, but I've heard some of the clubs are selling or providing footage to tabloids and (gossip website) TMZ," said an insider. Some of the clubs even have night-vision cameras, while others have cameras set up outside the entrance to stay on top of the situation.

"We welcome that," said a club exec. "We want every inch documented. You want protection from lawsuits and you don't want to see the casino's gaming license jeopardized." Cameras also allow establishments to keep tabs on customer service. But above all, they're an ever-present encouragement of good behavior. "The No. 1 reason you have it is it's a deterrent."

The growing technology is breathtaking, but not yet on the level of the once-popular NBC series *Las Vegas*, where the zoom lens could check the color of a high roller's pupils. Two of the biggest surprises: Few casinos added metal detectors after the 9/11 terrorist attacks, and security personnel are rarely armed.

Club strategies

It pays to have friends, and Las Vegas mega-clubs have adopted that as a strategy to boost the crowd numbers.

It's as simple as it sounds: Club giants Light Group and Pure Management Group have policies that require staffers to invite friends to the club, usually ten per night and "usually females, preferably hot females," said an insider.

Do the math. If you have a staff of 100, that translates into 1,000 invited guests a night "and you're going to look busy." Those who bring in the most guests get the best shifts, the best sections, and other perks.

There are repercussions if your guest list falls short. "You could get fired, written up, or get crappy shifts," said a spy.

Which brings us to the new term for cocktail servers. Now the job description is known as a "model/marketing/cocktail position."

"If we terminate servers for not having enough people on their list, we can say they were hired as cocktail marketing people," says a club executive. Truth be told, in some cases, "It's nothing more than a precaution in case a waitress gets a little tubby."

Guests usually love to be invited by the staffers because they can get inside the hottest clubs without paying a cover charge. "They usually just get in, unless it's a group of strippers. Then they'll get a bottle."

There's another sweet deal that allows big clubs to take advantage of their status as tenants: The casinos will pick up a heavy player's club tab and reimburse the club. (Sometimes, the host casino is strictly a landlord; others are passive partners after paying for the build-out of the club space.) Casinos know the longer they keep the high rollers on property, the better shot they have of them playing.

Another crowd-building strategy evolved with the popularity of social networking websites such as *MySpace.com*. Pure, for one, scheduled MySpace parties. A competitor added, "It was smart. We encourage our staffers to help promote themselves and our club by getting on MySpace."

In a superheated market, you've got to work every angle. At least one major nightclub group insists that its employees support their clubs on off nights. Being seen at a competitor's club has been known to raise loyalty questions, especially if there's an all-out war between the clubs.

Nightlife VIP services

With so many options and so little time to deal with lines that require two-hour waits, more nightlife VIP service companies are popping up. They cater mostly to tourists, executives, celebrities, and even locals who lack the connections or information to maximize the Las Vegas experience.

These companies have the connections at the most exclusive clubs, allowing their customers to bypass the line and gain immediate access so they can get their party started. Many reserve tables (remember, bottle service) for the ultimate nightlife experience. "Every situation is different and we create packages based on each client's needs and budget," said Chance McDaniel of *VegasVenues.net*, a referral-based company.

Another website, *Nightclubs.com* specializes in a ticketing system that provides customers with an "E ticket" guaranteeing expedited entry and no cover. The cost is comparable and oftentimes less than one would pay at the door, but no hassle or waiting in line. *Nightclubs.com* works with 78 clubs in Las Vegas and has expanded to other major cities including Miami, Chicago, and New York.

Job opportunities

If you are a young and beautiful female, the job opportunities in Las Vegas are endless. And not all of them involve taking off your top or working the pole.

Many of the dancers in major shows on the Strip moonlight as go-go dancers in the clubs, making $55 to $65 an hour. Modeling work of all varieties abounds.

The Palms hires cheerleaders for its Hardwood Suite in the Fantasy Tower. High rollers can leaf through a catalog of models they want to hire as cheerleaders for the basketball games in the $25,000-a-night super-suite.

At CatHouse inside the Luxor, scantily-clad models pose in windows out front and inside. Others go from patron to patron with a lingerie catalog. If you find something your wife or girlfriend might like, the dancers change into the outfit and dance in it on a nearby stage.

The bathtub and voyeur room models at Tao collect $50-to-$65 an hour, as do models who wear only body paint, for the most part, to various events.

Brittney Palmer, a cast member of Flamingo's *X Burlesque*, hauls in $600 as a ring girl at major boxing and UFC events. "I can make $400 to $600 a day at conventions," said Palmer, who works seven-to-ten conventions a year. "All you do is work in a booth, wear their clothes or shoes and just stand around and provide atmosphere."

It's no accident that many of the same stunners show up at party after party or VIP opening nights. All the major clubs "try to spice it up a bit with models," said Kent Henderson, owner of Best Agency. "They generally don't want to pay though. They offer a free table with bottle service, or dinner and a table in the club."

Some jobs are better than others. About 100 young models got last-minute calls to show up at Mandalay Bay's wave pool for a Kenny Chesney mini-concert that was being telecast during a cut-in for the CBS broadcast of the *2006 Academy of Country Music Awards* at the MGM Grand Garden Arena. Organizers didn't feel they had enough beautiful people among the regular hotel guests, so they made calls to local talent agencies seeking 100 more. The lucky gals received $175 each and got to watch Chesney perform.

Chapter 10 – The Best Gig in Vegas

A mong the most sought-after jobs in Las Vegas — up there with working as a nightclub doorman — is casino host.

"Everybody wants to be a casino host. When a job opens, the lines are unbelievable," a veteran host told me. It's not just the cash — $400,000 to $500,000 in salary — but the cachet.

Name another job where the biggest names in sports call you when they want to play a different game. Imagine having the power to send a corporate jet to pick up one of the richest men in the world. Or having a whale relying on you, after a run of bad luck, to approve an increase in his credit line.

Most top hosts have risen from the junior ranks, learning from the ground up. They answer phones, meet new customers, learn casino marketing. They learn at the entry level who gets comped and how much to comp them.

The pay isn't that great early on, but the deeper the database and the thicker the portfolio of wealthy customers, the more the money starts flowing. Some of the larger gaming companies, like MGM Mirage, reward top executive hosts with shares of stock as incentive to keep from losing them to rival properties.

"I've got a list of players who will follow me wherever I go," said the man we will call Mr. X, a host at one of the top properties, who must remain anonymous because of the sensitivities of his position.

Mr. X keeps in touch with his customers on a regular basis. Sometimes that means generating or receiving up to 100 phone calls, text messages, or emails a day.

So much of the job is about developing friendships. Having a gift of gab goes a long way. But just as important, "You have to know when to say 'yes' and 'no' the right way," he added. "You establish credit and comping. You're making decisions all day long."

It all starts with a credit line. For years, $100,000 has been the Mason-Dixon line for credit in Las Vegas, separating the real men from the boys.

Someone who wagers between $20,000 and $100,000 automatically gets comped with a room, food, and beverage. "You'll have a limit on food and beverage," said a source with intimate knowledge of the comping system. "Even with the $250,000 player, you can't go crazy (on the comps). It's the wine and champagne you have to watch."

With a $250,000 player, "You might let him spend $5,000 on dinner. You might do that one time per trip. If he buys a $1,000 bottle of wine, OK. Two thousand? OK. But you've got to watch it," because runaway perks eat up profit.

The bigger the player, the better the amenities

A $100,000 player qualifies for a penthouse, but you'd have to put up $250,000 to get into one of the villas or super-suites. The difference shows up not only in the square footage and views, but in amenities. Only six properties in town have those mega-suites, ranging from the MGM Grand's Mansion to the Palms' Fantasy Suites.

"Anyone who bets $25,000 a hand is a whale. Less than half of one percent bet at that level," a casino executive told me. "At $25,000, you've got a credit line of $1 million. At that level,

you can demand anything you want."

Among those who play in that rarified air: NBA icon Michael Jordan, who has carried a $2 million credit line for years. His running mate Charles Barkley weighs in at $1 million. So does Wayne Gretzky. Tiger Woods started out slow, at $100-to-$200 a hand. But since he started rolling with Jordan and Barkley, "he's moving up fast," to a credit line of $20,000 to $25,000 per hand, said an MGM Mansion spy. By the way, home run king Barry Bonds loves Vegas, but he doesn't gamble.

To land a whale, gaming companies send private planes over oceans to bring in business. If a big player flies in on his own jet, a trip that costs $60,000 to $70,000 for fuel, some casinos will kick in an airfare discount. "We'll pay half for the $500,000 player," a high-level casino exec told me.

But for the most part, a casino will stick with the five percent airfare rule. A $100,000 player might get $3,000 to $5,000 for an airfare discount. If he's a $250,000 player and plays to his line, "we would give up to five percent for his airfare, win or lose," said the executive. "But you don't offer airfare and discounts unless they ask."

Some hardship cases are known to ask for "walking" money, and some casinos still provide it.

Growing up in eastern Montana in the 1950s, I heard the name Benny Binion's name far more than Howard Hughes. Binion, the legendary owner of the Horseshoe, owned a cattle ranch near Jordan, not far from my hometown of Terry. My father, Charles G. Clarke, built livestock reservoirs for him.

Binion not only had a soft spot in his heart for cowboys, but he was known to buy a bus ticket home for many a Montanan who went bust.

I told that story to a local casino honcho and he said, "We've given out $500 'walking', knowing you won't get it back."

Above: Nicolas Cage, a fan favorite.
Photo: ☺Tostie14/Kevin Tostado
Below: *My Name is Earl* actress Jaime Pressly.
Photo: Craig L. Moran/*Review-Journal*

VIP host verdicts: The good, the bad, and just okay

You hear a lot about who's haughty and who's nice when Sin City's casino and VIP hosts start spilling their secrets (in confidence). Here's what a few of them have to say about some of Hollywood's hottest names:

The good

"Ray Romano and Brad Garrett paid for their own drinks during a 2007 visit to the Playboy Club at the Palms."

"You know who's a really good guy? Nicolas Cage. I've never seen him rude to anybody and he's willing to take pictures."

"(*American Idol*) Kelly Clarkson is just one great down-to-earth person. (Former NFL star, now broadcaster) Marshall Faulk's a really nice guy."

"Jenny McCarthy is really down to earth; Jaime Pressly, too."

UFC champ Chuck Liddell "blends in like any other person. He's really laid back."

The bad

"Kobe Bryant's arrogance is out of control. He's not cordial at all. He wants fans kept away from him. Not the nicest guy in the world to people."

"Matthew McConaughey is definitely in the top two of arrogance."

"Athletes have the tendency to expect things. The B-celebs come in thinking they're God-sent. All

Left: He's the tops!
Photo: Craig L. Moran/ *Review-Journal*

Below: Kobe Bryant at press conference for the NBA All Star game.
Photo: John Gurzinski/ *Review-Journal*

Opposite page: A bubbly Pamela with Tommy Lee.
Photo: Denise Truscello/Courtesy Planet Hollywood

Below: Kevin Spacey at *21* premier at Planey Hollywood Resort in 2008.
Photo: Denise Truscello/Courtesy Planet Hollywood

the B-celebs feel like they should be comped. Most of the A-listers are people that really don't have a lot of expectations other than getting in quick and getting the normal attention."

"Soap opera people are the worst. They really think they deserve everything, even to the extent of requesting a security guard."

The just okay

"Gene Simmons desperately needs attention. At the same time he's a gentleman, but he has this persona he has to live by."

"Kevin Spacey is okay, but he was doing some weird stuff, grabbing guys' asses."

"Porn stars aren't that bad."

"Kid Rock is real reserved. Doesn't socialize that much."

"Pamela Anderson is the sloppiest celebrity I know. She'd come in Pure and be so wasted that one of her breasts would be out. She reminds me in the way she behaves and parties of Anna Nicole Smith. When they were partying, I don't think either knew where they were. She and Anna Nicole were always in La La Land."

Saved by the Bell principal Dennis Haskins, who played Mr. Belding, "really wants everything for free."

CHAPTER 11 – Bad Blood and Fighting Words

Las Vegas has long been a battleground for rival millionaires, mobsters, and entertainers.

Almost 40 years before billionaires Steve Wynn and Sheldon Adelson dueled over who had the tallest hotel, two other Las Vegas icons, Howard Hughes and Kirk Kerkorian, fought a similar turf war.

When Kerkorian decided to build the world's largest hotel with the International (now Las Vegas Hilton) in 1969, Hughes countered by buying the tallest building in town: the 31-story space needle-like Landmark Hotel, directly across the street from Kerkorian's monstrosity.

A decade later, the "Battle for the Aladdin" between Wayne Newton and Johnny Carson hit the headlines.

Here are some of the best celebrity tiffs of the new millennium:

Can I autograph this door I kicked down?

One of the best celebrity feuds in years played out in Sin City in 2007 when Kid Rock twice went after Tommy Lee.

Still seething from a marriage to Pamela Anderson that disintegrated within months, Rock was gunning for Lee, the presumed spoiler, on New Year's weekend, when all three were in town for the final days of 2006.

When Anderson showed up with celebrity bodyguard Chuck Zito, it was a sure sign that she expected trouble. Rock had made his feelings loud and clear three weeks earlier, during a Vegas visit shortly after the separation from Pamela. While partying at the Hard Rock Hotel

Opposite Page: The Landmark Hotel, one of several properties owned by Howard Hughes.
Photo: Toru Kawana/ *Review-Journal*

Below: Rockers Kid Rock, seen above and Tommy Lee, seen below share more than a fondness for graphic t-shirts.
Photo: ☺Lightgazer

Photo: ☺Joe Telling

with Kenny Chesney and Jason Giambi, he was seen wearing a t-shirt with the message "Bros Before Hos."

That wasn't a chip on Rock's shoulder, it was the whole damn Sequoia.

When he returned for a guest DJ appearance at Jet nightclub on New Year's Eve, Pamela was across the street, guest-hosting at the Venetian's mega-club Tao. To make the triangle complete, Lee was performing at the Hard Rock Hotel. I was hearing rumblings that Rock was out for blood and I led my December 31 column with this paragraph:

"Las Vegas' James Bond-themed New Year's Eve couldn't be more fitting. The nation's hottest nightclub scene has become a battle royale, and the potential for celebrity drama rarely has been higher."

The ink was barely dry on the newsprint when Rock showed up on the 11th floor of the Hard Rock at about 6 a.m. with two NFL-sized bodyguards. They weren't calling it a night; they were looking for Lee's suite.

Here's professional poker player "Hollywood" Dave Stann's account of what happened next:

"Someone was trying to kick down my door. I got up and looked through the door (peephole). It was two huge linebacker dudes screaming, 'Tommy's in there.'

"I told them, 'There's no Tommy in here.'"

Stann said he called security. By the time help arrived, the thugs "had left size 14 boot prints and splintered the door," said Stann, who added he and his girlfriend were "freaked out" by the incident.

Stann said the floor only can be accessed by a VIP room card. His room was two doors down from the Hard Rock's penthouse suite.

Hard Rock publicist Spencer Villasenor emailed this explanation: Rock was "looking to settle a dispute over ex-wife Pamela Anderson." But when Rock realized he was at the wrong door, "the gentleman that he is, he signed an autograph for the apparent fan" and left.

Stann said security told him they found two men at his door and they were Rock's bodyguards. And no one was offering an autograph. When I called Villasenor back to double-check the facts, he reiterated that Rock was at the door.

Eight months later, Rock and Lee were both again in town for the *MTV Video Music Awards* at the Palms and they went out of their way to stay far apart. They had rooms in opposite hotel towers, and it wasn't by accident.

Below: Pammie in her jammies with Rick Solomon in a suite at Planet Hollywood Resort.
Photo: Denise Truscello/Courtesy Planet Hollywood

Rock, who had earlier spurned Anderson's overture before going down the red carpet, could not have missed seeing her going over to Lee's table and sitting on his lap. A spy at the table said the tension had already been elevating because Lee "was pushing Kid Rock's buttons. When Rock saw Lee at the table, he said, 'You should get out of here.' Diddy (Sean Combs) was sort of instigating it, too. Tommy stood up and was showing some attitude and Kid (got up and) smacked him."

As security moved quickly to break up the ruckus that unfolded in full view of MTV cameras and remove Lee from the venue, Rock turned to a friend and said, "You got cash on you? Bail me out."

In the aftermath, Lee told the cops he was seated when Rock tapped his shoulder and "sucker-punched me." A few days later, he referred to Rock as "Kid Pebble" and the punch as a "bitch slap." When Lee pressed charges, Rock was cited for misdemeanor battery, but was not arrested.

Within a few days, showman Jeff Beacher of Beacher's *Madhouse* was on Howard Stern's radio show offering a $1 million winner-take-all grudge boxing match between the two rockers at the Hard Rock. He had no takers.

Pamela Anderson: Las Vegas is more faithful than a husband

Better known for her marriages than a career, Pamela Anderson looked to Las Vegas for a bust-out break.

With more curves than the Hollywood hills, Anderson should have been an easy sell in a city that embraced all things sexy.

Opportunity came calling in 2004, when Scores, the New York strip club popularized by Howard Stern, offered a 10-year, $1 million-a-year deal for its new Las Vegas location. Pam would get a percentage of Score's net profits as well. All she had to was show up every four months, sip champagne and hang out for two hours.

It looked like a no-brainer, until she unveiled her ideas at a meeting with the club owner Dennis DiGori. Anderson showed up at the meeting with her friend David LaChapelle, the gay fashion photographer who designed the visuals for Elton John's *The Red Piano* show at Caesars Palace (Anderson is featured prominently in the video for "The Bitch Is Back.") She told DeGori that she wanted the club renamed The Burning Bush, and proposed a super-sized sign of herself out front — á la Vegas Vic, the 40-foot neon cowboy above Fremont Street.

One more thing, she said. The sign would be large enough that cars could drive between her legs for a car wash. Using your imagination, you can visualize the rest.

DeGori had reservations, and Anderson eventually bailed on the idea, saying she "didn't want to hurt her reputation," because, after doing a sex video with Tommy Lee, she didn't want to give anyone the wrong impression.

Her car wash concept had similarities to what Anderson, during a February 2004 interview, told me she had planned for the interior of the strip club she envisioned. Club goers would enter by passing through a giant pair of legs.

In what sounded like an addendum to the Bad Ideas file, the PETA supporter added that she wanted the club named LaChaPamela, adding it would reflect her personal tastes: a vegetarian menu, soy milk cocktails, and no leather or fur on the staff.

Despite these non-starter schemes, there were signs she was going to be spending more time in Las Vegas. She picked up a suite at Panorama Towers, where her neighbors would include Leonardo DiCaprio and Tobey Maguire.

For a while Anderson gave Britney a run for her money when it came to Sin City controversy. She kept using the Strip as a gossip-generating backdrop for her love life.

In July of 2006, she was back in town, promoting a poker site at the World Series of Poker two days before her marriage to Kid Rock. They had been engaged since 2002, when Kid popped the question during a desert sunset near Primm, 30 miles outside of Las Vegas. Kid's pal, Uncle Kracker, dressed as Elvis, drove up with the engagement ring in a pink 1961 Cadillac Eldorado Biarritz. It wasn't a good sign when the Caddy blew an engine a couple of miles away.

The relationship overheated too, but they patched things up and she was on her way to St. Tropez for the wedding when she stopped off in Vegas.

"I see the light and I feel like I'm finally free," she told the media at a World Series of Poker press conference.

Five months later, her marriage was over when she returned to Las Vegas to host a New Year's Eve countdown, accompanied by celebrity bodyguard Chuck Zito. She clearly had an inkling that things could get messy, and they did.

I was tipped that weekend that Kid was gunning for Lee, and sure enough, it hit the fan at 6 a.m. December 31, when Rock and some of his goombahs tried kicking in the door of an 11th floor Hard Rock Hotel suite, daring Lee to show his face.

Anderson summed it up with this entry in her website: "A rock star scorned . . . completely childish threats . . . that's why my friend Chuck Zito is with me."

She finally became a Las Vegas headliner in the summer of 2007. Her first gig on the Strip turned out to be as a well-paid magician's assistant to Dutch illusionist Hans Klok, who producers wisely realized could use a boost in marquee value on the Strip. Anderson replaced

Opposite page: Pam moves on. Anderson with Rick Solomon, her husband of three months.
Photo: Denise Truscello/Courtesy Planet Hollywood

Carmen Electra in Klok's *The Beauty of Magic* at Planet Hollywood. Her best performance, however, was off-stage, where she went to great lengths trying to promote the notion that a romance had bloomed with the magician, who was fairly obviously gay (and later came out with *Q* magazine, a local gay publication). But no one was buying it, especially the ticket-buying public, and the show disappeared in six months.

The proof was in the pudding when Anderson walked the red carpet at the *MTV Video Music Awards* at the Palms with Klok, (Anderson's handlers insisted that he be introduced as her "boyfriend"), and three days later Pamela was on Ellen DeGeneres' show, announcing she had gone ga-ga over a new man.

Four weeks later she was walking down the aisle at romantic Planet Hollywood casino with Rick Salomon, who was best known for his sex tape video with Paris Hilton that earned him a reported $10 million.

Few were surprised when reports surfaced that the perfect couple was shopping a reality show within weeks, or that she filed for divorce less than three months later.

Brad and Pamela: No love lost

Brad Garrett and Pamela Anderson won't be sharing a dais any time soon.

Garrett, best known as hangdog brother Robert on *Everybody Loves Raymond*, was emceeing a roast of poker ace Doyle Brunson at The Mirage in 2006 when he instead savaged Anderson, who was two days away from her short-lived marriage to Kid Rock. It was brutal. The room fell silent as Garrett cracked on the bride-to-be for her super-sized curves and sexual history.

A fuming Anderson walked off the dais after making the shortest speech of the night. As she headed toward the door, a member of her entourage yelled, "When

are you going to get funny, Brad?" The tense exchange continued when the six-foot eight-inch comedian called out Pamela's defender, saying, "Come on. When you're done shooting up, we'll go toe-to-toe." In the next breath he referred to the entourage member as, "Tommy Lee's afterbirth."

Sources said Garrett was asked by Anderson's people before the roast to "lay off" her. "It was agreed by the promoters, the comedy writers, and Brad's agent and management that Pam would not be made the subject of the roast," a member of Anderson's camp told me. (Perhaps Garrett was still caught up in the spirit of the infamous Comedy Central roast of Anderson the year before. But this time, she was in Las Vegas to launch her *pamelapoker.com* website in conjunction with Brunson's *Doylesroom.com*.)

The next night, Garrett got the evil eye while attending Elton John's show at Caesars Palace. During a video featuring Anderson's stripper pole dance, which accompanies John's "The Bitch is Back," a group of Anderson's loyalists in front row seats turned around in unison and glared at Garrett two rows back.

"We were not amused with Brad's roast (of Anderson)," said Larry Edwards, a long-time Tina Turner impersonator. "We were letting Brad know that Pamela is our queen," Edwards said.

Renaissance rivalry revisited

A modern-day version of a legendary Renaissance rivalry is unfolding on what Donald Trump calls "the hottest corner in the world right now."

The colossal building boom along Las Vegas Boulevard "goes to my argument that Las Vegas is the Venice of the 21st century," local author Michele Jaffe (*Bad Kitty*) wrote in an email.

Jaffe is a Harvard grad who studied comparative litera-

ture and wrote a book on the Renaissance period. She has her own perspective on the unprecedented era of one-upmanship waged by rival billionaires Trump, Kirk Kerkorian, Steve Wynn, and Sheldon Adelson.

Above: "You're Higher!" Trump's buildings take the lead.
Photo: Denise Truscello/Courtesy Planet Hollywood.

"In Venice during the Renaissance, rich men flexed their fiscal muscles through architecture, building larger and more sumptuous palazzi (palaces)," Jaffe said. "Competition played itself out in the wow-inducing facades they put up on either side of the Grand Canal, the 'Strip' of Venice."

Trump's "hottest-corner-in-the-world" reference came during an interview at the topping-off ceremony for the first of his two 64-story residential towers. It is no coincidence that Trump's 645-foot towers eclipse

Wynn's 614-foot Wynn Las Vegas and is on track to top Adelson's Palazzo, which tops out at 55 stories and is also at 614 feet, which would make Trump's building — take that! — a full nine feet taller.

But the phallic war doesn't stop there: Wynn's Encore, when completed next year, will take over as the tallest at 653 feet. But I'm told the owners of the $5 billion Plaza planned for the New Frontier site will end up — surprise — between 650 and 680 feet.

All this reminds Jaffe of the storied competitions played out in the 1550s between the scion of the well-established Tiepolo family and an up-and-comer named Girolamo Grimani. The latter fell hard for Tiepolo's daughter, but when he went to ask for her hand in marriage, the father scoffed at the brash newcomer, saying (reportedly), "I'd never give my daughter's hand in marriage to a nobody who doesn't even have a house on the Grand Canal."

Rebuffed but fired up, Grimani "is said to have given what, at the time, was the insult to end all insults," Jaffe wrote. "Building on the fact that glass was a luxury commodity at the time, he declared, 'You just wait. I'll build a palace where every window is bigger than the door of your palazzo.'

"And he did. The imposing marble facade of the Palazzo

Grimani stands exactly across the Grand Canal from the Palazzo Coccina-Tiepolo."

Jaffe concludes, "Although it happened 450 years ago, it's a very Vegas story: Rivalry played out through marble and glass."

Adelson and Wynn have taken shots at each other for years, but the feud intensified in 2008 when Adelson told freelance writer Steve Friess that Wynn's "time has come and gone." The height of Adelson's new Palazzo next door to the original Venetian "was a big part of the argument why he didn't like us," Adelson told Friess in an interview for *USA Today*.

Wynn didn't respond to Adelson's jabs, but Wynn made it clear in an earlier interview with me that he missed the kinder and gentler days of Las Vegas.

"We never had jealousy and sniping until relatively late in the history of the town. And it came from newcomers, not guys who have grown up in the business. That's a Sheldon Adelson thing," he said. "We didn't have it before. It was just the opposite; we all went and gambled at each others' openings. There's no animosity there, there's no jealousy. There may be a 'Wow, look at that, there's something to shoot at, let's do better than that.'

"But it's sort of healthy. We've all done well because we've been with each other here, not in spite of each other. The secret of Las Vegas is the fact that we've all been here," Wynn said.

He compared the animosity of today with the day he sold his Mirage Resorts to Kirk Kerkorian's MGM for $6.4 billion. He and Kerkorian "went out and celebrated when we made our deal," Wynn said.

Below: Mr. Nice Guy, Kirk Kerkorian.
Photo: Jeff Scheid/ *Review-Journal*

"He was a customer at the Nugget, played blackjack with me. Came down for bread pudding in the buffet. There's not a speck of jealousy in that man."

Fight night at Piero's

A bitter relationship boiled over at Piero's Italian Cuisine before two NBA coaches stepped in to break up a brawl in 2007.

The altercation involved Sandy Murphy and Benny Behnen, grandson of Horseshoe founder Benny Binion.

By the time two unidentified coaches broke up the melee, Murphy had a clump of hair ripped from her scalp as she was trying to escape from her assailant.

The incident occurred the night before Murphy appeared in District Court seeking to gain possession of part of the estate of the late Ted Binion, Behnen's uncle and the man Murphy was accused of murdering in 1998. An eyewitness said words were exchanged when Murphy's party and Behnen's group were seated at nearby tables in Piero's most popular bar area.

When scuffling broke out, Murphy moved away from the trouble and was near the kitchen exit when she was cornered by a young man.

"Sandy wanted to get out of there," said her attorney, Herb Sachs. "Behnen saw her, targeted her, and punched her, kicked her, and grabbed her hair."

Fred Glusman, owner of Piero's, confirmed that Murphy and Behnen were involved in the melee, which occurred in the area where scenes from the movie *Casino* were filmed. "Sandy got hit. Don't know who hit her, it all happened so fast," said Glusman, who was not at the eatery at the time.

"Three fights broke out. It was like the old wild, wild West," added Glusman. "Some NBA coaches broke it up." By the time police arrived, "it was all over," he added.

Murphy, a former stripper, and her one-time lover, Rick

Tabish, were charged in 1999 with drugging and killing Ted Binion in a plot to obtain his assets, including $7 million in silver buried on rural ranch land. They were convicted in 2000 and sentenced to life in prison, but their convictions were overturned by the state high court. Murphy and Tabish were acquitted of murder after a second trial in 2004.

After Murphy's hearing before Judge Elizabeth Halverson, Murphy approached William Fuller, the 80-something benefactor who paid many of her legal fees.

"She kissed him and said, 'Did you hear what happened?'" According to *Review-Journal* reporter K.C. Howard, "Then she pulled a clump of hair out of her purse and said, 'This is mine.'"

It's not the first time Behnen was involved in a battle at Piero's.

In August 2000, he allegedly mixed it up with high-stakes gambler Bob Stupak, former owner of Vegas World, over Stupak's attempt to cash some casino chips at Binion's Horseshoe. Behnen's mother, Becky Behnen, operated the Horseshoe after Ted Binion was barred from running it.

Piero's also was the scene of a federal raid in 2005, when agents, one armed with a submachine gun, stormed the tony restaurant and arrested retired New York City cops Louis Eppolito and Steve Caracappa. They were jailed in connection with the murder of Gambino crime family associate Eddie Lino.

Caught in the middle

You might be surprised to know I ended up in the middle of one of the uglier feuds in show business — Johnny Carson vs. Wayne Newton — many years before I started this job.

One day in late 1980, the telephone rang in the Associated Press office in San Diego and a gentleman identified himself as Carson's attorney, Henry I. Bushkin. The name automatically registered. It was the man Carson always referred to as "Bombastic" Bushkin on *The Tonight Show.*

He explained that he had seen my byline on an AP story out of Las Vegas about a recent Newton news conference.

"We may be calling you to testify," said Bushkin.

In January 1980, an agreement had been reached to allow Carson and partners Ed Nigro and National Kinney Corp. to buy the Aladdin for $105 million. It was to be renamed Johnny Carson's Aladdin.

But the deal collapsed in May. In October, I covered a news conference in which Newton, then just 37, announced he would file a libel lawsuit against *NBC News* the next day. NBC was alleging that organized crime was involved in Newton's recent purchase of the Aladdin for $85 million.

Earlier, Newton had been quoted as saying that Carson, a rival bidder for the Aladdin, could have been behind the NBC story.

Newton couched his comments at the news conference: "If I accused him (Carson), I'd be as wrong as NBC was last night. In my opinion, he doesn't have anything to do with it."

Newton won a $5.2 million libel suit against NBC for linking him with organized crime. I never heard from Bushkin again.

A federal court overturned the award in 1990, ruling the reports were not deliberately or recklessly false.

For reasons that aren't entirely clear, Newton, who had just had a heart scare that forced him to cancel a series of engagements, reignited his animosity about the late Carson in December 2007, during an interview with CNN talk-show host Larry King.

The bad blood began, he said, when Carson began joking "a lot" that Newton was gay. "I had done his show many, many times and considered him a friend of mine," said Newton. "And all of a sudden, a whole new brand of humor started to be displayed by him. And he was in that humor questioning my masculinity."

When all efforts to reach Carson failed over a year and a half, Newton said, "I went to see him."

Newton went to NBC in Los Angeles, found Carson in his office meeting with producer Freddy de Cordova and asked de Cordova to leave the room.

"And I said to Mr. Carson, 'I don't know what friend

Below: Newton in rehearsal.
Photo: John Gurzinski/*Review-Journal*

of yours I've killed, I don't know what child of yours I've hurt, I don't know what food I've taken out of your mouth, but these jokes about me will stop and they'll stop now or I will kick your ass.'"

Newton told King, "I'm going to say something I've never said on television, Mr. King. Johnny Carson was a mean-spirited human being. And there are people that he has hurt that people will never know about. And for some reason at some point, he decided to turn that kind of negative attention toward me. And I refused to have it."

When King asked Newton if the confrontation hurt his career, Newton said, "In retrospect, no. I think, probably, there was a time that it could have hurt my career. But I think ultimately, the whole thing that evolved later on, around 1980, where I was accused of fronting for the mafia and being a member of the mafia and then being extorted by the mafia and all of that, all of that emanated from Johnny Carson's influence."

Friends no more

Harry Morton and Brandon Davis, members of two famous families, grew up as best friends in Los Angeles.

Davis was a grandson of billionaire Marvin Davis, former owner of 20th Century Fox, the Pebble Beach Company, the Aspen Ski Company, and the Beverly Hills Hotel.

Morton's father, Peter Morton, founded the Hard Rock Cafe chain and built the Hard Rock Hotel in Las Vegas.

The falling out came when Davis, upon turning 21, quickly blew through several hundred thousand dollars in credit at the Hard Rock Hotel, then owned by Peter Morton.

According to insiders, young Davis lost it all within weeks, and after paying off $240,000, went into rehab.

Don't Mention It

It will be many moons before the NFL and Las Vegas make peace. The relationship hit a low point when the NFL insisted that NBC move its *Las Vegas* series with James Caan from Mondays to Fridays because the NFL wanted nothing to do with promoting Las Vegas during Sunday Night Football.

The NFL put a clause in the contract with NBC that forbids the mention of Las Vegas, which would block the network from next-night promotion of one of its primetime shows. The feud started when the NFL cracked down on Super Bowl parties around the city.

Above: James Caan, star of *Las Vegas* the TV series.
Photo: Denise Truscello/Courtesy Planet Hollywood

Tom Arnold, hired by Davis' family to be his sobriety coach, asked the Hard Rock Hotel to retire the remaining debt and bad-mouthed Harry's dad for demanding immediate payment. Even the family rabbi reportedly called, asking for mercy.

In the end, Davis' mother, Nancy, sold her son's car and other possessions to pay the debt.

Harry and Brandon never patched things up.

For my next trick

You get the feeling David Copperfield would like to see Penn Jillette disappear.

Reacting to Copperfield's 2007 announcement that he plans to make a female audience member pregnant on stage "without sex," Jillette cracked, "The only way Copperfield can reproduce is with a cheesy magic act."

Copperfield countered, "If his reputation were as big as his gut, he wouldn't need to include me in his press release."

That exchange occurred months before Copperfield came under federal scrutiny after a Seattle woman alleged he raped her at his home in the Bahamas. The FBI raided a Las Vegas warehouse used by Copperfield on the same night that the Rio threw a party for Penn & Teller, celebrating their five years at the hotel.

Below: David Copperfield performs immaculate conception?
Photo: Louis Lanzano/AP

Catfight at 'Crazy Girls'

Things got a bit crazy one night at the *Crazy Girls* show at the Riviera.

Angela Stabile (formerly Sampras), a former *Crazy Girls* dancer who started a rival show called *X Burlesque*, says she was confronted by management and removed from a booth by security late in the show.

Stabile said Karen Raider, associate producer for *Crazy Girls*, came to the booth and demanded to see her former colleague's ticket stub.

Raider "grabbed my arm and tried to pull me out of the booth," said Stabile who performed in the show for most of the 1990s via email.

Raider's version: "I told her she's a fired dancer and 'You have to go.' Security took them out. She knows she's been 86'ed from Day One.

"She's just hyping her new show," Raider added in a telephone interview.

Stabile said she was told she was being kicked out "because I stole their girls and that I copied their numbers! I have never stolen any of their girls. No one owns the dancers; they are not a piece of property or slaves. I have always tried to do everything different from *Crazy Girls*.

"Talk about the pot calling the kettle black! *Crazy Girls* is a direct copy of (famed French cabaret) *Crazy Horse Paris*," she added.

And a Feud of my own

I would be less than candid if I didn't mention the rivalry with Timothy McDarrah, the hitman the *Las Vegas Sun* brought in for a bumpy two years to compete with my column.

I didn't have to wait long to figure out which road he was going to take.

He started out on the high road. His first email to me was a classy, I-respect-your-work-hope-we-can-be-friends message. I was going through some difficult medical challenges at the time he arrived in the fall of 2002. I had undergone cancer surgery and numerous complications, including a mysterious inability to walk for almost three months. During that time I hit rock bottom. My legs had deserted me; my voice was all but gone as my health continued to deteriorate. I appreciated McDarrah's kind words and I immediately told him so. He was a veteran of the *New York Post*'s famous "Page Six" gossip column and son of respected *Village Voice* photographer Fred McDarrah. I told him I looked forward to competing with him and afterwards, sharing war stories over beers. I was fascinated with the legendary New York gossip battles.

A day or so later, he made a tour of the morning radio shows and we got a much clearer picture of what road he would be heading down. The day he made the radio stops, I had a blurb in "Vegas Confidential" that Oscar-winning director Steven Soderbergh, in Norway to receive an honor, confirmed to the Norwegian media that an *Ocean's Eleven* sequel was in the works. I attributed it and was happy to have it. McDarrah's take? He told the deejays that he was aware I was "sick" but, c'mon, I was going to have to do better than that now that he was in town.

I let him know what I thought about it two or three days later. I was talking with local publicist Steve Flynn when McDarrah came up and introduced himself in a hallway while we waited for the post-fight interviews following the Oscar De La Hoya-Fernando Vargas fight at Mandalay Bay.

It was a short and less-than-sweet conversation. "That was some low-rent shit you said on the radio. I hope you feel good about that," I told him.

"I'm sorry you feel that way," he said, shrugging his shoulders before walking away.

It was the last time I had anything to say to him, other than hello. I did send him an email a year or so later, after he reeled off a burst of fabricated items. My message was basic and brief: "Tim, there is so much A-list material in this city, you don't need to make it up."

As Robin Leach has said on so many occasions, celebrity coverage in this city is "like standing under an apple tree with a basket."

But McDarrah, some 20 years my junior, didn't want my advice: "You don't want to get in the ring with me, old man," he fired back in an email.

Soon he was Topic A on the gossip list — generating it, not covering it — for his loud and obscene party behavior, hitting on the TV babes and public relations cuties he worked with. Then there was the shaky reporting, heavy on unattributed "phantom" quotes. It was the kind of self-destructive behavior that kills careers, and it wouldn't be the first time the Vegas pace and competitive pressures took their toll.

The editors at the *Sun* finally had their fill of him, but *US Weekly* hired him as their lead "Hot Stuff" gossip writer in the fall of 2004. It made a lot of sense. The Vegas celebrity scene was white hot and McDarrah took a lot of territorial knowledge with him when he returned to his home turf of New York City. When he left Las Vegas, many of us were convinced *US Weekly* would have their hands full vetting his reports. If a sports book was taking bets, I would have taken one year as the over/under "line" for how long he would make it, for a lot of reasons.

But pedophilia wasn't one of them.

McDarrah was arrested nine months later for soliciting

sex from an undercover federal agent posing on the Internet as a 13-year-old girl. A U.S. Attorney's office press release detailed the exchanges, saying McDarrah wrote that he would tutor her and give her "sex lessons."

McDarrah was convicted in December 2006 after an eight-day jury trial in New York, and in April 2007 was sentenced to six years in prison.

I chose not to write one word about his downfall, until now.

Sands

A PLACE IN THE S

Sands

DEAN & JERRY
MARTIN LEWIS
THE FOUR STEP BROS.
IN THE LOUNGE
LOUIS JORDAN

LOUIS JORDAN AND HIS
TYMANY FIVE
RUBEN AND THE GUADALUPES BOYS
ERNIE STEWART TRIO

continuous
entertainment
nightly
in the lour

CHAPTER 12 – It's Vegas, Baby!

Youtube and cell phone cameras changed just about all our notions of what we consider public and private behavior. While society sorts out the consequences of that sea change, it's safe to say Las Vegas was in on the ground floor of blurring the lines between celebrities "performing" and merely acting up. From the days of the Rat Pack starting the party on the Copa Room stage and then wrapping it up in the lounge at dawn, we continue to monitor that cherished tradition of stars being stars even when they're not on the clock.

Opposite page: The Sands' Copa Room was home to the Rat Pack.
Photo: Review-Journal archives

How do you like him now?

You can't keep a good man down. Before the New Frontier closed, Toby Keith was a regular at country nightclub Gilley's during National Finals Rodeo week. In 2005, Keith walked in and sat down at his favorite barstool in the front section before joining Ricochet and Thunder Road for well over an hour on stage. One night earlier, Wayne Newton joined Keith and Night Ranger on stage for a long jam of "Gimme Some Lovin'" at Keith's own I Love this Bar inside Harrah's Las Vegas. In 2004, he rode the mechanical bull at Gilley's in the wee hours during a break from performing for hours with Gilley's house bands, as well as with Ricochet and Daryle Singletary.

Below: Keith jamming with Newton.
Photo: Courtesy of Harrahs

Dawn patrol with Tom Jones

Of the legendary headliners still working Las Vegas, no one since Sammy Davis, Jr. is known for more after-hours, drop-in appearances than Tom Jones.

It's not usual to find him at any number of local off-Strip clubs, putting on marathon shows until dawn, while sharing the stage with lesser-known entertainment pals.

Below: Cook E. Jarr appears at Harrahs.
Photo: Craig L. Moran/ *Review-Journal*

The first one I was tipped off about was in August 2000. Back then, I wrote:

"Most nights Cappozoli's restaurant serves up everything Italian. Early Sunday, they were serving up nonstop slices of Old Vegas. At 2:30 a.m. the legendary Tom Jones walked in with Cook E. Jarr. Three hours later, Jones was still on stage, a champagne glass in one hand and a microphone in the other, belting out Elvis and Sinatra hits, along with his own chart-busters such as 'Delilah.'"

"This was a throwback to the old-Vegas days," said Harrah's headliner Clint Holmes. Also joining in the fun were musical impressionist Bob Anderson, comedian Dennis Blair, and Elvis impersonator Pete Willcox, along with Holmes' musical sidekicks Bill Fayne and Pat Caddick. "You couldn't walk through the bar," Homes added. "I left at 5:25 a.m. and Tom was still onstage."

"He's got iron lungs," Jarr told me after one of the marathon sessions. "I call him the Caruso of rock and roll. He lays into every note. Perhaps an iron liver as well; Jarr recalled one instance when Jones invoked a Welsh custom that no liquor be left on the table.

Over the next several years, there were Jones sightings at The Manhattan, Olio (the MGM restaurant later renamed Fiamma), Casa di Amore (which owner Bobby Capozolli later renamed De Stefano's), and Café Martorano in the Rio, where owner Steve Martorano rewarded him with a $1,200 bottle of Hennessy Paradis cognac.

Above: Jones and Jarr performing late into the night.
Photo: Courtesy Photo

Pure imagination?

Johnny Depp, wearing his Willy Wonka costume from the just-completed *Charlie and the Chocolate Factory* movie, while making a stop at the AquaKnox restaurant at the Venetian in July 2005. The shutterbugs went wild.

Lucky them

Guests at the Hard Rock Hotel weren't feeling so lucky when they had their sleep interrupted in the wee hours by someone practicing piano in a nearby suite. Turns out the culprit was actress Drew Barrymore, who was in town filming *Lucky You.*

Barrymore, cast as a struggling singer who hooks up with a poker player (Eric Bana), was brushing up on her piano skills. The not-so-tickled guests were allowed to move to other rooms.

Lucky dog

Hugh Hefner's live-in gals and the stars of the reality show *The Girls Next Door,* Holly Madison, Bridget Marquardt, and Kendra Wilkinson, were spotted shopping at the pet fashion boutique Lush Puppy at Mandalay Bay in 2007. Madison went ga-ga over a doggy coat that resembles one of Hef's smoking jacket, with a silky lining and velvet exterior, as well as some gourmet cigar-shaped doggy treats.

Left: The stars of the TV Show, *The Girls Next Door.*
Photo: Cara Roberts

Hot pink

Dennis Rodman, who never met a fashion statement he didn't like, wore a pink camisole with blue silk parachute pants to Tangerine nightclub at Treasure Island in 2007.

Below: Pretty in pink and ink?
Photo: Courtesy Pure

Below: *Ocean's Thirteen* co-stars George Clooney and Don Cheadle, seen here, hooped it up in Vegas.
Photo: Craig L. Moran/ Review-Journal

Honk if you loved *Con Air*

Nicholas Cage received an ovation after trying his musical skill on the alphorn at the Hofbrauhaus in April 2006. He was with his wife Alice and six-month old son Kal-el.

Court cons

George Clooney beat Don Cheadle two games to none in one-on-one basketball in the Palms' Hardwood suite, where Clooney stayed during the 2007 Las Vegas premiere of *Ocean's Thirteen*.

Lookin' for adventure

Taking a break at the Mt. Charleston Hotel after a Harley ride were Jay Leno, Keith Urban, and the country duo Montgomery Gentry.

Airborne

NASCAR driver Michael Waltrip, taking the inaugural ride on the Stratosphere's latest thrill ride, Insanity, during the VIP party in 2005. He also rode the Big Shot and X-Scream rides on top of the tower.

The dollar is weak

King Carl XVI Gustaf of Sweden happened to be in Light on the Bellagio club's "Gold Digger Night," when fake money is handed out to VIPs. That caused a ripple of chuckles among all the king's men. The monarch was in town to check out the restored classic Shelby GT he purchased.

All hail

To mark the 40th anniversary of Caesars Palace in 2006, former MTV host and Playboy centerfold Jenny McCarthy was carted on a Roman litter by Centurions to the outdoor toga party. She was wearing a Marciano-designed toga. Eat your heart out, Cleopatra.

Is that Rachel?

Jennifer Aniston put on a memorable show for some instant "friends" at Ivan Kane's 40 Deuce burlesque club inside Mandalay Bay during the 2005 New Year's weekend. She climbed onstage and rocked the house with a dance exhibition for her then-boyfriend, Vince Vaughn.

Above: No private dancer.
Photo: KM Cannon / *Review-Journal*

Above: The Stardust was part of the Vegas skyline for 48 years.
Photo: Courtesy Boyd Gaming

Viva Paula!

American Idol judge Paula Abdul joined the cast of the Cuban revue, *Havana Night*, onstage for the finale at the Stardust in August 2005.

Special K

A pep talk by Duke basketball coach Mike Krzyzewski highlighted opening night at Michael's restaurant, when the legendary gourmet room was transplanted from the Barbary Coast to the South Point in 2007.

Krzyzewski and his wife Mickie are Vegas regulars who had frequented Michael's restaurant in the Barbary Coast (now Bill's Gambling Hall) for years. After flying in specifically for the opening of the new location, Krzyzewski asked if he could say a few words to the staff after dinner.

"He gave a pep talk, saying how great it was that our team stayed together over the years, and he related it to basketball and life," said maitre d' Jose Martel.

The pep talk ended with Coach K and the staff joining in a champagne toast.

Krzyzewski is such a Vegas fan that he opted to bring his family — including a son-in-law who was home on break from serving in Iraq — on a previous trip rather than attend the 2006 NCAA Final Four in Indianapolis.

Elvis and Shelvis

NBA great Reggie Milller and his hoop star sister Cheryl Miller dressed up as Elvis impersonators for a TV segment during the broadcast of the 2007 NBA All-Star Game broadcast from the Thomas & Mack Center in Las Vegas.

Shooting the bull

Former Los Angeles Dodgers manager Tommy Lasorda, who has skippered World Series winners and Olympic Gold medal efforts, found himself in a different arena during the 2005 Professional Bull Riders finals. He was asked to fire up the participants with a motivational speech before the PBR finals at the Thomas & Mack Center.

Below: Lasorda meets fans at a Las Vegas 51s minor league baseball game.
Photo: Craig L. Moran/ *Review-Journal*

Wrong game for 'snake eyes'

Vince Gill's fear of snakes went to a terrifying new level during a pro-am golf tournament in Las Vegas. Gill said he was on the first hole at Cascata, a private club owned by Harrah's Entertainment. After coming upon a snake, Gill stumbled and fell. The snake was within striking distance, but Gill could not regain his footing. Finally, he managed to get away without injury and went on to birdie the hole.

Below: Gill won't be seeing the film *Snakes on a Plane* anytime soon.
Photo: KM Cannon/ *Review-Journal*

Red headed stranger indeed

Roy Hammock's dead-on impersonation of Willie Nelson has been fooling folks for years.

His uncanny resemblance has created some ticklish situations, said Hammock, 70, a fill-in with the *Country Superstars Tribute* at Fitzgerald's.

A few years ago, he stopped in a biker bar in Coeur d'Alene, Idaho, with some friends and got cornered by a big-as-a-house biker who insisted on going outside, saying, "I got some good stuff." Hammock stalled and tried sneaking off, he said, but got caught and had to fake his way through imbibing in the wacky weed.

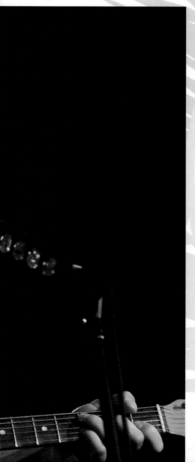

He met the real deal about eight years ago, shortly after giving up his convention meeting-planner career to become a Willie lookalike.

During their chat, Hammock promised Nelson he would never do anything to embarrass him. Nelson's response: "I hope you have as much fun being me as I do."

Luck be a lady

Miss America organizers made it clear they didn't want the contestants at the gaming tables, but the rule didn't apply to a very lucky cousin during the 2006 pageant. Amanda Fleishmann stopped at the Aladdin's Free Pull slot machine and with her single pull, won a new Toyota Scion. The irony here is that her cousin, Miss Montana, Sophia Steinbeisser, told me the day she arrived in town that she had been advised by her family to steer clear of "the Sin City stuff."

Jailhouse rock

Elvis impersonator Trent Carlini was all shook up after being ticketed for flashing a police badge. He was attending a fight at Mandalay Bay when security stopped him and asked him for a ticket or a credential. He showed them a badge. Big mistake. Carlini went on to win NBC's *The Next Best Thing*, a talent show for celebrity impersonators, and was the people's choice in a *USA Today* survey tied to the best-Elvis competition at Graceland in 2007.

Quality backup

LD Miller, a 12-year old harmonica whiz in the *Buck Wild* revue at the Sahara, came away from a meeting with BB King with a standing invitation. During his 2006 backstage meeting at the Stardust with King, Miller told the blues legend where he worked. When King learned *Buck Wild* was topless, the blues icon told Miller to call anytime and he would fill in for him.

I asked the pre-teen if being backstage in a topless show presented problems. Nah, he said, "My mom keeps me away from that. I got me a puppy now."

CHAPTER 13 – Only in Vegas

Ho's there?

During the conversion of the Aladdin to Planet Hollywood, work on the new resort's exterior sign suspiciously stopped for more than a few hours when the wording got to "Planet Ho." It was the devilish sense of humor of Robert Earl, founder of the themed eateries and new casino derived from them.

Opposite page: Earl celebrates the opening of Planet Hollywood with Bruce Willis.
Photo: Denise Truscello/Courtesy Planet Hollywood

Take your cubic zirconia elsewhere, sir

OPM nightclub at the Forum Shops at Caesars Palace separated the *playuhs* from the *players* at the Ballers Ball during the NBA All-Star Weekend in 2007. A certified jeweler was at the door, with testing equipment and eyepiece, to determine if the bling was the real thing. "If it isn't, you don't get in," said Branden Powers, OPM marketing director. Celebrity jeweler Johnny Dang showed up wearing more than $1 million in jewels, with his own private security to keep an eye on them. The club turned away more than 100 people whose jewelry failed to pass the test for authentic bling.

Above: Guy Laliberte, no tie required.
Photo: Courtesy Cirque du Soleil

Not a fan of the *Star Wars* prequels

Actress Natalie Portman was turned away at the Monte Carlo's brew pub in 2007 when she couldn't produce an I.D. Portman, 25, tried to convince the doorman who she was, but to no avail. She was in town with Norah Jones to film scenes for *My Blueberry Nights.*

You gotta speak French, A-Rod

New York Yankees' star Alex Rodriguez didn't have the stripes to enter Tangerine nightclub at Treasure Island during a November 2004 visit. It wasn't a dress code violation or a behavior issue.

It turns out Tangerine was closed for a party being thrown by Cirque du Soleil creator Guy Laliberte, who was throwing a private bash for the cast and crew of *KÀ*, the Cirque du Soleil production at the MGM Grand.

Recognize those showgirls?

Tyra Banks' showgirl debut ranked up there with some legendary catwalk catastrophes. With her daytime-talk show camera crew filming every shaky step, Banks tripped twice during her appearance while wearing a rhinestone bra and g-string in the opening number of *Jubilee!*, the long-running topless revue at Bally's. First her exotic headpiece fell off and she lost her balance while trying to catch it. "She managed to get across the

Above: Modeling easy, being a showgirl not so much. Tyra Banks with from left Adriana Lima, Heidi Klum, Alessandra Ambrosio and Gisele Bundchen.
Photo: John Locher/ *Review-Journal*

stage, but tripped on the other side," said my spy.

Actress Vivica Fox dressed in full showgirl regalia for the 25th anniversary show of *Jubilee!* in 2006. ABC's *Dancing with the Stars* camera crew followed her throughout the night, including her fox trot in the finale with Stars partner Nick Kosovich.

It's doubtful anyone remembers another *Jubilee!* "sighting." Heidi Klum was only 15, four years away from the launch of her career and legally too young to see a topless show in Las Vegas. But with a little help from her parents, the German beauty got her first taste of Sin City fashion at *Jubilee!*

"My parents sneaked me. I was really too young, but

No Bra Required

"Stuff like this you don't even dream of in Romania," said topless entertainer Roberta Lorincz. The call came out of the blue from a Las Vegas modeling agency. Would Lorincz, former lead ballerina for the Romanian National Opera, serve as a body double for Keira Knightley?

Lorincz, 28, leaped at the opportunity. Knightley had backed out of a love scene in *Domino* because she didn't feel comfortable showing her body. "Coming from Europe, it was not uncomfortable for me," said Lorincz, who had temporary tattoos applied to her neck and had to wear her waist-length black hair under a wig that resembled Knightley's short hairstyle.

Knightley was cast as Domino Harvey, who walked away from her career as a Ford model to become a bounty hunter. Harvey, who died of a reported drug overdose, was the daughter of British actor Laurence Harvey.

Lorincz got to spend seven hours working next to Knightley during the *Domino* shoot at the Valley of Fire.

my parents dressed me up to look older," Klum recalled at the sneak preview of Tao Beach, the topless pool at The Venetian inaugurated in 2006.

She loved that first Vegas adventure, back in the late 1980s, "especially the Bob Mackie costumes."

They Forgot about Blue Hawaii

When NBC's *Today Show* weatherman Al Roker delivered a forecast from the pirate ship at Treasure Island's Buccaneer Bay, he recruited some local talent from across the street. As Roker predicted snow in the northeast,

members of the Blue Man Group slathered shaving cream on a map of the region. When he forecast rain in the Midwest, they handed Roker an umbrella, and squirted the area with super-soaker waterguns. For the finale, when Roker predicted sunshine in Florida, the Blue Men put on their shades and passed out boat drinks with Jimmy Buffet music playing in the background.

Below: Blue Man Group livened-up Al Roker's weather forecast. **Photo:** KM Cannon/ *Review-Journal*

Trump's dude ranch
Eric Trump, Donald Trump's son, learned the Trump name doesn't always open doors. Young Trump was

turned away from Light, a Bellagio nightclub (now called The Bank), while celebrating his 21st birthday in 2005 because his party of 15 guys was too large. Light's chick-friendly policy usually limited parties of men to six to keep the female ratio high.

Holy high roller!

As celebrity sightings go, this is a first on several levels: Six of the nine Catholic cardinals in the United States showed up in Las Vegas in 2007 for their annual fund-raiser for Catholic University. The traditional gathering, a first for Las Vegas, featured many of the seven cardinals who serve as archbishops of U.S. dioceses. With that many cardinals assembled in Las Vegas, it was wise to "bet on red," quipped local show producer Myron Martin, who spotted them.

The question that has to be asked: How did Sin City beat out St. Louis, home of the 2006 world champion Cardinals, as the host site?

Advice on wheels

MSNBC's *Hardball* host Chris Matthews got some advice from his Las Vegas limo driver.

"Embrace the superficiality," the limo driver told Matthews, who was on his way to interview Palms owner George Maloof in a $25,000-a-night sky villa at the Palms' Fantasy Tower.

Matthews' first trip to Las Vegas didn't include a private limo. "I drove out here in 1971 to see some friends after leaving the Peace Corps," Matthews told me.

On the way from Utah, he picked up a hitchhiker, "an old hobo who had been on the road since the 1930s. He insisted I spend a Saturday night in Las Vegas. The thing I remember most was that he was just so optimistic."

Can you go for a master's degree too?

You knew it was inevitable. David Saxe, producer of
V — The Ultimate Variety Show, in June 2006 opened
what he billed as the first striptease class in town, allegedly for professionals but just as much aimed at visitors
looking for new kicks to tell the folks at home. He calls
it "Stripper 101."

Don't let them near the booze aisle

Tim Dahlberg, Las Vegas-based sports columnist for
the Associated Press, passed this along as a candidate
for the quintessential only-in-Vegas moment: He was
shopping at an Albertson's grocery store miles from
the Strip when he heard music that was not the usual
piped-in variety.

He made his way to the source: "There's a Rat Pack
band. Frank was singing in the meat department, and
Sammy and Dean were doing their thing. All in tuxes,
raising funds for a charity.

"I asked the cashier how long they were booked, and
he said, 'Way too long.'"

Drinks for all my friends

UFC fight champ Chuck Liddell, flashed all ten badass
fingers at a Rain bartender during a Kid Rock concert
at the Palms hotspot in April 2006. As Rock sang, "Bad,
Bad Leroy Brown," Liddell passed out Southern Comfort
and lime juice shots to nine of his new best friends.

It's my birthday, too!

When it comes to birthday blowouts, Las Vegas takes
the cake.

Celebrating a birthday in Sin City is as popular as the
booming wedding business and the bachelor/bachelor-
ette road trips. A Las Vegas birthday offers all the heady
extras: a gambling getaway, star-chef dining, big shows,

Above: Liddell showed some
Southern hospitality.
Photo: KM Cannon/ *Review-Journal*

Opposite page: Pamela celebrates the big 4-Oh!
Photo: Denise Truscello/Courtesy Planet Hollywood

Below: Shall we dance?
Photo: Craig L. Moran/*Review-Journal*

a forest of stripper poles, and non-stop partying.

Let's cakewalk through some notable celebrity celebrations:

As fantasy birthday parties go, it would be hard to top Elaine Wynn's 2005 soiree. Her husband, Steve, the billionaire casino mogul, chose her birthday as the opening date of the $2.7 billion Wynn Las Vegas.

The party included an appearance by Elaine's favorite opera star, Renee Fleming, who made a grand entrance at Alex restaurant by singing "Summertime" while descending the stairs modeled after the set from the Broadway hit *Hello Dolly*.

And if having film icon Elizabeth Taylor and dozens of other stars at your birthday party wasn't enough, the topper came when hunky Hugh Jackman, the evening's entertainer, coaxed Elaine into a dance.

Taylor didn't do badly for her own 75th birthday in February 2007. A New Orleans-themed party at the Ritz-Carlton at Lake Las Vegas included Siegfried and Roy, the Wynns, Debbie Reynolds and daughter Carrie Fisher. For those who still remember their big feud, Reynolds long ago forgave Liz for marrying Eddie Fisher, who had divorced Reynolds to marry Taylor in Las Vegas on May 12, 1959. Accompanying Taylor, who was in a wheelchair, were her children, Michael Wilding, Christopher Wilding, Elizabeth Todd, and Maria Burton.

A tickled-pink Pamela Anderson celebrated her 40th birthday on July 1, 2007 with wall-to-wall pink flowers, a sparkler-topped pink cake, and enough champagne to float a small boat.

The party started as soon as Anderson and illusion-ist Hans Klok finished their second performance of *The Beauty of Magic* at Planet Hollywood Resort. Klok presented the Playboy icon with a rare book written by Houdini. More than 100 friends, including her parents and ex-husband Tommy Lee, attended the private party hosted by Planet Hollywood owner, Robert Earl, in the mezzanine-level nightclub that had not yet opened to the public.

Before K-Fed became Fed-X, Britney Spears arranged a Vegas-style birthday show for him at Tao Asian Bistro in March 2006. First, a plus-sized female impersonator dressed as Cher sang, "If I Could Turn Back Time." Then Cher was joined by a little person dressed as Bono for a duet of, "I Got You Babe." (The performers were Steve Daley and Shorty Rossi of the Sahara's since-closed *Buck Wild* show.)

David Copperfield's 50th birthday party on September 15, 2006, in-cluded a cake from Pure Nightclub sculpted in the shape of the Exuma archipelago in the Ba-hamas. The illusionist bought an island retreat there for a reported $50 million. (The getaway was pulled into the news pages in October 2007 when a Seattle woman accused Copperfield of sexually assauting her at his home there.)

And you thought a champagne toast was a splurge. Poker ace Phil Ivey bought a bottle of $13,000 Louis XIII Cognac at the birthday party of NHL agitator Claude Lemieux in the Caramel lounge at Bellagio.

Tom Jones serenaded Sylvester Stallone at an early 60th birthday party at Planet Hollywood in June 2006. Witnesses included California Governor Arnold Schwarzenegger, Bruce Willis, James Caan, John Travolta, Donald Trump, and Tony Curtis, who was celebrating his 81st birthday.

Cameron Diaz and Justin Timberlake opted to celebrate his 25th birthday (January 31, 2006) on the stylish side, dining at Wynn Las Vegas' Bartolotta Ristorante Di Mare before heading for Pure Nightclub and a performance of the original Pussycat Dolls.

Below: Holy cannoli! "Rocky" is sixty!
Photo: Denise Truscello/Courtesy Planet Hollywood

I Brought a Doctor's Note!

Barry Manilow abruptly ended his show after one song on September 16, 2006 at the Las Vegas Hilton. He apologized to the crowd and explained that he was heading to double hip surgery.

Celine Dion missed several performances at Caesars Palace after suffering a sinus reaction to a smoke machine during her appearance at the World Music Awards at the Thomas & Mack Center in September 2004. It ended up being a five show cancellation.

For Jack Osbourne's 21st birthday celebration in November 2006 at Stack inside the Mirage, the birthday cake had a Thai theme. That's because Osbourne, a former party hound who took after his famous father Ozzy, found his spiritual side during rehab in Thailand two years earlier.

Sister Kelly Osbourne's 21st birthday party in November 2005 wasn't so ascetic. Jeff Beacher, producer of Beacher's *Madhouse*, had a little surprise for her. Upon being presented with a sheet cake, Osbourne watched 21 little people march onstage to salute her.

Dennis Hopper celebrated his 70th birthday (a month late), at Tao in June 2006, enjoying a sparkler-topped tiramisu cake with his wife, bodyguard, and a CineVegas film festival group that included Helen Mirren and her husband, director Taylor Hackford.

Pop singer Aaron Carter was the victim of his twin sister's sweet revenge. While celebrating their 17th birthday in 2004 at Planet Hollywood restaurant in the Forum Shops at Caesars, Aaron got a face full of bright red frosting when Angel, his sister, pushed his head into their birthday cake. It was a payback for what he did to her on their 16th birthday.

No cake request is too extreme for Las Vegas chefs. Famed architect Frank Gehry, known for his quirky, unorthodox perspectives, got an appropriate birthday cake during a 2005 lunch at the MGM Grand's posh Mansion. Gehry, who was celebrating his 76th birthday, was presented with a chocolate cake structure that, instead of having a roof where it belonged, had it attached on the side of the building. Gehry was commissioned to design the similarly asymmetric Lou Ruvo Alzheimer's Research Center in downtown Las Vegas.

Paris Hilton had Stavros Niarchos' three-tiered birthday cake at Fix inside the Bellagio topped with a figurine

Vegas goes dark — really dark

Lounge legend Cook E. Jarr was minutes into his 2004 New Year's Eve gig at the Rio's Mardi Gras-themed Masquerade Village when the power went out. "I was singing 'Get Down Tonight,' and it goes pitch black," the colorful singer recalled. The only light he saw for the next 20 minutes was from his 'butt light," a powerful flashlight he shines on notable derrieres and cash redeemer machines.

Champagne celebrations fizzled temporarily as skittish revelers at the Rio, the Palms, Barbary Coast, and Flamingo wondered if they were in an *Ocean's Eleven* scenario or worse.

"My first thought was terrorism," confessed Jarr, who described it as one of his most stressful nights as a performer.

Palms owner George Maloof was at the Playboy Mansion in Los Angeles when his cell phone started crackling with calls.

The Palms' Rain nightclub, with almost 2,000 partiers, was being emptied, he was told, and ghostbar was a ghost town. Some 400 ghostbar occupants were led down the 40 flights of stairs before the power was restored 45 minutes later and the revelry resumed.

Back at the Rio, the property's costumed fruit-topped character Rio Rita was stranded on one of the masquerade village sky floats and had to be rescued with a rope ladder.

"Just another boring New Year's Eve in Vegas," said Madeline Weekley, Rio spokeswoman at the time. The cause of the power outage was mylar New Year's Eve balloons hitting a power grid.

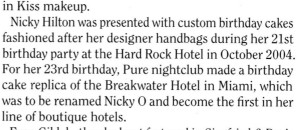

of a kite surfer, his favorite sport. At his 56th birthday party in 2005 at the Palms ghostbar, Kiss frontman Gene Simmons was presented with a birthday cake decorated with a likeness of his tongue-flicking face in Kiss makeup.

Nicky Hilton was presented with custom birthday cakes fashioned after her designer handbags during her 21st birthday party at the Hard Rock Hotel in October 2004. For her 23rd birthday, Pure nightclub made a birthday cake replica of the Breakwater Hotel in Miami, which was to be renamed Nicky O and become the first in her line of boutique hotels.

Even Gildah, the elephant featured in Siegfried & Roy's show for two-plus decades, had a birthday party and an unusual cake. The four-ton ceremonial Thai elephant celebrated for years by chowing down on a four-foot high cake made of carrots and fruit with a straw-filled center. Topping the cake was multi-colored Cool Whip. Gildah died in 2005 at age 57.

Pop singer Avril Lavigne spent most of her 21st birthday week in 2004 at the Palms with then-fiancé Deryck Whibley, lead singer of Sum 41. She was spotted playing the slot machines while snacking on popcorn and pizza and washing it down with a dirty martini.

Jenny McCarthy and her sisters, Joanne and Amy, their parents, and sixteen gal-pals decided to be more conspicuous. They all wore hot pink wigs while celebrating Amy's 21st birthday at Stack restaurant inside the Mirage in July 2006. Afterwards they partied at Jet, where they put on a stripper pole show.

For her own 34th birthday on November 1, 2006, McCarthy welcomed Prince to her VIP bed section at Pure nightclub in a French maid outfit. Would I ruin the image to mention it was a Halloween party? Also there, NASCAR star Dale Earnhart, Jr. with Robbie Gordon

Above: Vegas is a mecca for those celebrating their 21st birthday such as Avril Lavigne.
Photo: ⓒ Amy-Wong.com

Opposite page: Comedian Rita Rudner with daughter at Cirque de Soleil show *Mystère* at Treasure Island (TI). *Photo:* Norm Clarke

and others, all dressed up as characters from *Reservoir Dogs*.

It's no fun to have your dad tag along on your 21st birthday, unless some call him Bond: James Bond. Pierce Brosnan accompanied his son, Christopher Harris, on a 21st birthday tour in October 2003 that took in clubs at the Luxor, Palms, and MGM Grand, where they joined parties with *American Idol* contestants and staff members. Singer Billy Idol opted for a sweeter evening for his daughter Bonnie's 16th, taking her to Picasso restaurant at Bellagio.

Harrah's headliner Rita Rudner hosted a princess party for daughter Molly's fifth birthday in June 2007 at Little Divas. "Hair, nails, and a fashion show. I'm sure it's going to come up in therapy at some point," said Rudner, who bought Molly a miniature castle. More than a dozen little princesses were in attendance, she said.

No princes? "There will be no princes," said Rudner, "for at least 25 more years."

Circus Circus

Gabriella Versace, the lead in the Rio's since-closed *Erocktica* revue, had an audience member get a bit physical. A man climbed on stage, threw her over his shoulder and proceeded to spin her around on two occasions. "He was five-feet tall and I'm 5 foot 8 inches. I felt like we were doing a circus act," Versace said.

Chapter 14 – Guess who?

Planet Hollywood carpet photo: David G. Schwartz

Sometimes I can only go so far. I can't tell you the answers to these questions — well, maybe if you buy me a drink some day — so don't bother turning the book upside down for an answer key. But I thought you might at least get a kick out of the guessing game.

What headline-generating blonde was caught in the act on the floor of a Palms elevator? Her torrid tryst with a centerfold started sizzling in a poolside Jacuzzi, went horizontal in the elevator, and ended up in a suite, when they spent the night and a full day. . . .

When it comes to the dealers' Hall of Shame, this guy is a shoo-in. They're still talking about the time this well-known baseball star was mistakenly paid $5,000 and walked when asked to return it, as a pit boss read him the riot act. . . .

What local casino kingpin, known for his legendary libido, once dressed up for a Halloween party as the Dirty Old Man from *Rowan & Martin's Laugh-In?* . . .

There are worse things than being a bad tipper. A cheater, for one. A former NBA tough-guy and Vegas regular is infamous at Las Vegas tables for "past posting," the sneaky practice of adding chips after a bet. This guy is known to play for $2,000 to $6,000 a hand. One night, he had $2,000 on the table when the dealer turned away momentarily, only to look back in time to catch the guy illegally pressing his bet to $4,000. When the dealer called him out, the ex-player lied. Management ran the tapes and sure enough. The dealers know him for something else: Talking big. Never a night goes by when this well-past-his-prime player isn't insisting

Opposite page: The tables are turned on Norm by Kirsten Haglund, who went on to become Miss Ammerica 2008.
Photo: Tom Donoghue/Courtesy Planet Hollywood

Tee-totalers

This classic golf story came from the PGA tour stop at the Tournament Players Club at Summerlin: An employee at the club was curious when he heard someone rattling around in the liquor cabinet in a private lounge.

Peering around a corner, the employee spied one of the big hitters in golf, a guy known for his love of the high life, helping himself to six shots of Louis XIII cognac, which goes for $100 to $200 a shot at many Strip properties.

After placing the shots on a tray, the "big spender" strolled off to treat his buddies in the clubhouse. What he didn't know was that management, aware that someone was tapping the good stuff, filled the cognac bottle with cola.

loudly that he could return to the NBA and pull down $5 million a year. . . .

What casino executive made a call, after seeing NBC's *Las Vegas* series, to complain that his name should have been given to James Caan's character? . . .

What country star with a drug problem took a local topless beauty to lunch, and at the conclusion said he wanted to get together with her later that night for some ecstasy and the ultimate in bad taste? . . .

What former topless revue babe changed her last name to that of a sports star she pursued with passion? . . .

What blonde-loving casino exec asked for ten of them to join his group after he had a big night at the gaming tables? After showing his buddies a good time, the extra-generous exec doled out $55,000 to be split ten ways. . . .

What one-time perennial Top Ten college football team, not from the West Coast, agreed to have a number of top players flown in as a last-second favor? The reward: A trip to one of Pahrump's brothels. Big hint: the team color is commonly associated with cathouses. . . .

What well-known manager for a megastar entertainer plays poker under an alias for security reasons? . . .

What rising political star, not from Nevada, has been risking it all with his wild trips to Las Vegas strip clubs? . . .

Name the World Series-winning, now-retired big league manager who was so smitten with one of Vegas' most famous transgender headliners that he flew "her" to New York City for a weekend? She was so convincing that many inside the local entertainment community didn't know for years that she was formerly a he. . . .

What front man for a major rock band settled into a Bellagio suite with his girlfriend for a wild night when their plan went awry? After an hour or so of being hand-

cuffed to the bed, he asked his gal to get the key and
free him. She didn't have the key, she said. They realized the key was elsewhere, so she dressed and drove
off to retrieve it.

About the Author

"Vegas Confidential" columnist Norm Clarke has been covering the Las Vegas celebrity scene for the *Las Vegas Review-Journal* since 1999. Prior to his move to Sin City, he spent 15 years in Denver, where he was an award-winning sportswriter at the *Rocky Mountain News* before moving into the man-about-town column in 1996.

The Montana native had a 12-year stint with the Associated Press in Cincinnati, San Diego, and Los Angeles, most of it as a sportswriter and newsman. He was The AP's coordinator of coverage for the 1984 Summer Olympics in Los Angeles. He lives a few blocks off the famous Strip at Las Vegas Country Club with his girlfriend, Cara, and beloved puppies Rumor and Scandal.